Preparing for the SOL

World History Test

World History and Geography
A.D. 1500 to the Present

Richard Weber
Supervisor of Social Studies 6–12
Newport News Public Schools, Virginia

AMSCO

Amsco School Publications, Inc.
315 Hudson Street, New York, N.Y. 10013

The author dedicates this book to Virginia's social studies teachers,
who are meeting new challenges with talent, enthusiasm, and determination.

Editor: William H. Johnson

Cover, text design, illustrations, maps, photo research, composition: A Good Thing Inc.

Please visit our Web site at:
   www.amscopub.com

When ordering this book, please specify:
R789W or Preparing for the SOL World History Test: A.D. 1500 to the Present, Softbound

ISBN 1-56765-661-7

Printed in the United States of America

1 2 3 4 5 6 7 8 9 10   09 08 07 06 05 04 03

Contents

Introduction

The purpose of this book is to help students achieve success on the Virginia Standards of Learning (SOL) end-of-course test in World History from A.D. 1500 to the Present. In this regard, the book has two obvious strengths. First, the content is drawn from Virginia's *Curriculum Framework for History and the Social Sciences*, which is the source of the SOL test content. Second, the practice tests are designed according to the state blueprint for the test, and they simulate the ways in which each SOL is tested.

Equally important is the book's alignment with the organizational plan of the Virginia standards. The standards are an attempt to capture world history in all of its richness and complexity. However, many teachers and students have found the standards' organizational plan to be both novel and perplexing. This book provides the details that make the design clear.

Some Notes for Teachers

Your students will benefit from the book's attention to the five critical issues of SOL test preparation:

- Understanding the historical context of events and trends

- Identifying the key questions associated with each time period
- Seeing the influence of geography on history
- Locating events in space and time
- Practicing SOL content in the SOL test format.

Understanding the historical context. The World History SOLs were written to promote historical literacy. That is, they were designed to specify what students need to know about world historical events, ideas, people, and documents in order to be informed participants in shaping our nation's future. Historical literacy does not require students to memorize a vast number of details, to be pulled out at any moment. What it does require is a grasp of key generalizations. If your students can answer the key questions posed by each SOL, they will succeed on the SOL test.

Despite the significant amount of specific content in the World History SOLs, most students will use their general sense of world history to answer many of the questions. This book provides **Setting the Scene** and **Summing Up** features for each SOL. These features give students the "big picture" of each historical period.

v

Key questions. The Virginia State Resource Guide provides some Essential Questions that a student would need to be able to answer to be successful on the given standard. Our Key Questions go beyond those of the state guide and even more closely reflect the issues raised in the SOLs. By providing clear and concise answers to these questions, this book explains just what the students need to know for the SOL test.

The influence of geography on history. The introduction to the History and Social Science Standards of Learning notes that "History should be the integrative core of the curriculum, in which both the humanities (such as art and literature) and the social sciences (political science, economics, and geography) come to life." Geography comes to life in this book through the author's insights into the influence of geographic features on the outcomes of conflicts, the development of trends, and the relations of nations.

Location in space and time. How frustrating it is to know about a historical event but be unable to place it on a timeline for a test question! Or to be unable to choose the correct location for the event when given a map! A student needs not only to know the time periods and the locations of events but also to acquire a mental timeline and mental map to place them in. Remember, the SOL test is primarily a history test, but it tests students' understanding of the geography behind the history as well. That is why this book contains a section on geography skills, and why the text itself highlights the time and space locations at every opportunity.

SOL practice questions. Through careful study of the sample questions for the World History test, the released test questions from previous SOL tests, and the specifications used to construct the test, the authors have learned the keys to SOL test-taking success. SOL practice questions are provided for each chapter. Plus, two complete simulations of the World History from A.D. 1500 to the Present test are provided for a good check on your students' preparedness for the real test.

Advice to Students

With good planning, success on the SOL Test in World History from A.D. 1500 to the Present is an achievable goal. This test-preparation book provides the right content, with the right strategies, for success. Students, for best results, we suggest that you start at the first chapter. Read the SOL, then Setting the Scene. See if you can answer the Key Questions for the chapter. Writing down some notes about how you would answer each question will help you see how clear the issues are in your mind. For any Key Question that gives you trouble, read the answer provided in the text carefully, taking additional notes. Answer the Chapter Review questions, see how you did, then either check back to the text or move on.

Do not waste time on what you *do* know. When you have worked all the way through the book, take a full hour to do the first SOL Practice Test. The test will not be timed when you take it, but you will not be able to work on it forever. After an hour, you will start to tire out, so see how well you can do in that time. On another day, give yourself a full 90 minutes to do the second SOL Practice Test. See how the additional time affects your score and plan your pace for the actual test accordingly. By now you will know exactly what SOL content gives you trouble, and you can focus on it. Copy the relevant material from the test prep book into a small notebook, and keep that handy to look at in the last days before the test. Now you are ready for success!

Chapter

1

Historical and Geographical Skills

Virginia Standard of Learning WHII.1

The student will improve skills in historical research and geographical analysis by

a. **identifying, analyzing, and interpreting primary and secondary sources to make generalizations about events and life in world history since A.D. 1500.**

b. **using maps, globes, artifacts, and pictures to analyze the physical and cultural landscapes of the world and to interpret the past since A.D. 1500.**

c. **identifying geographic features important to the study of world history since A.D. 1500.**

d. **identifying and comparing contemporary political boundaries with the location of civilizations, empires, and kingdoms from A.D. 1500 to the present.**

e. **analyzing trends in human migration and cultural interaction from A.D. 1500 to the present.**

Standard WHII.1 a, b.
Sources of information

Key Questions for Standard WHII.1 a, b

1. **What sources of information are used to make generalizations about events and life in the world since A.D. 1500?**

2. **How are maps, globes, and other geographic tools used to analyze the world and interpret the past?**

1. HISTORICAL SOURCES

Written records and pictures. A huge number of written records exist with which to study modern world history. The Gutenberg printing press of 1450 was not a new invention: The Chinese invented this type of printing press much earlier. Gutenberg's press, though, began the mass production of books and other printed articles that has continued to the present day. Both **primary sources** (those written during the time being studied) and **secondary sources** (those written later to describe that time) have increased in number.

1

The number of sources produced was not the only change brought by the printing press. Compared to most handwritten sources, printed sources are much easier to read. A biographer of Benjamin Franklin has described the challenge of interpreting handwritten sources as "sometimes overwhelming," even though Franklin and his colleagues had better handwriting than most people have today.

In the middle of the 19th century, photographers began to record images of both daily life and major events, as artists did in drawings and paintings. Mathew Brady's pioneering photos of the Civil War have been uniquely valuable to historians (despite criticism of Brady for rearranging scenes of battle casualties before taking the pictures).

Typewriters and improved printing presses continued the trend toward clearer, more numerous records. More recently, tape recorders, photocopiers, video recorders, computers, and a host of other electronic information-storing devices have provided means to record almost anything that happens and to study it later.

Though historians are glad to have all of these kinds of records, the vast volume of records can create problems. A character in Kurt Vonnegut's novel *The Sirens of Titan* reports that in the distant future historical records become so extensive that they threaten to push human beings off the planet. (To regain needed space, the historical record from the death of Christ to A.D. 1 million is reduced to a single line of text.) While Vonnegut's "records crisis" is fanciful, it illustrates a feature of historical study of modern times. Modern historians need to sift and sort immense quantities of information while managing to "see the forest for the trees."

Still, some events of modern times—those intended to be kept secret—offer only scant evidence. Some of these events must be studied in much the same way as those from the distant past. The facts behind mass murders in Bosnia and other places have come to light mainly through careful study of physical evidence, such as human remains and **artifacts** (human-made objects).

Modern artifacts. The Industrial Revolution increased production of goods beyond what people in ancient and medieval times experienced. As a result, artifacts of modern times are extremely numerous. Virtually anything produced in a time period, from a teaspoon to a skyscraper, has something to tell about the period.

As with written records, the large number of artifacts of modern history can make their interpretation difficult. Which tools, games, artwork, and articles of clothing are typical of modern times? If a historian collected the items from your room at home, would these artifacts provide a useful picture of young people today? Which of these artifacts do you think will stay in good enough condition to be studied at the end of the 21st century?

Judging authenticity. With both written records and artifacts, it is important to establish that they are what they are claimed to be. Documents are usually judged correctly, though there have been exceptions to this rule. In the 1980s, a fake Hitler diary fooled numerous experts, as have some faked documents with importance to the Mormon Church. Photographs are especially suspect in the computer age, since one of the features of electronic information storage is the ability to change stored information easily. As a result, digital photography can produce whatever images the photographer wants to show. At the same time, new technology has given historians, using chemical and photographic processes, effective tests of authenticity for some kinds of documents.

2. MAPS AND GLOBES

Maps and globes show geographic information. Globes have the advantage of being shaped somewhat like the earth and not show- ing the distortion that comes from represent- ing its three dimensions in two dimensions on a piece of paper. The various methods of rep- resenting the round world on flat paper, called

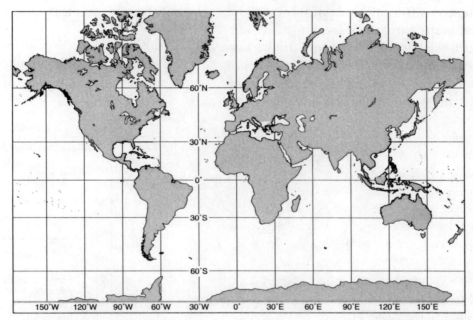

Mercator projection (above).

Robinson projection (below).

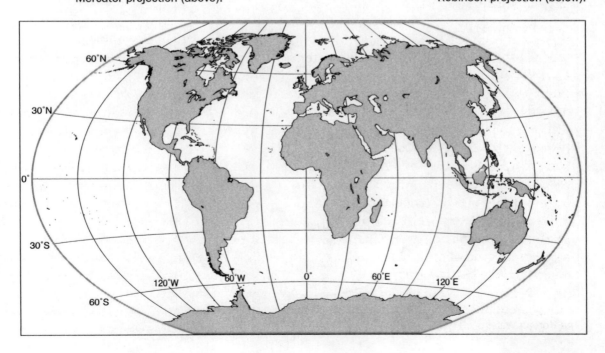

projections, all distort the true sizes and shapes of the physical features to some extent. On the SOL tests, maps of the world will use one of the projections on page 3.

Geographers use different types of maps to represent different kinds of information. **Political maps** emphasize human-made features such as national borders and cities. **Physical maps** emphasize the natural features of land and water. On the SOL test, you will see physical and political maps. The features on these maps will be selected to give you enough information to answer the question and no more, which is why the SOL maps are called *simplified* maps.

For some questions you will be asked to identify features on the map, as in this question:

1. On this map of the Korean War, what does the line marked by the number 3 represent?

   A. the farthest penetration of UN forces into North Korea

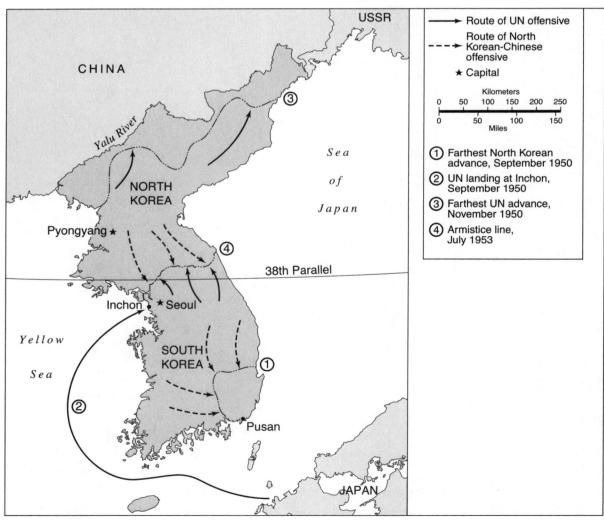

The Korean War.

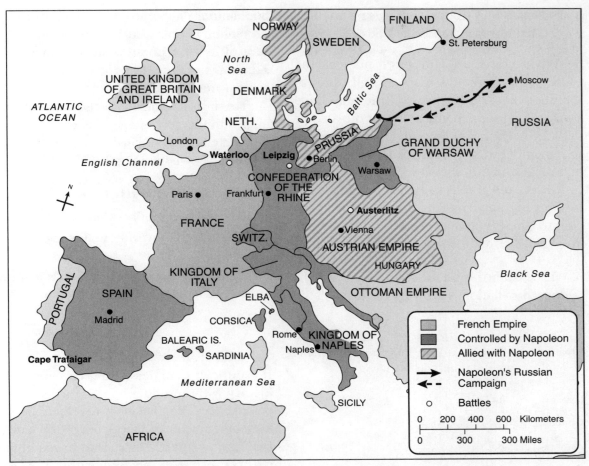

Europe before the Congress of Vienna.

B. the original border of China and South Korea

C. the Armistice line at the war's end

D. the path of the retreating UN forces in 1951

Look at the map on page 4 to answer this question.

Some questions will ask you to interpret arrows on a map. Such questions dealing with movements of ethnic groups, military troops, or trade products will usually require some historical understanding as well as map reading.

For example:

2. Using the map of Europe above, choose the correct description of Napoleon's Russian campaign.

F. The attack was to the east from Prussia to Moscow, and the retreat retraced this route going west.

G. The attack was into Prussia from the east, with supply routes running back to Moscow.

H. The attack was to the south of France, then northward to Russia.

J. Napoleon's troops went by ship on the Mediterranean and Black Seas.

When you see a simplified map on the SOL test, examine the map carefully and remember that the features on the map have been chosen to help you arrive at the answer without helping you too much. You will need to remember what you have learned about the historical situation shown on the map.

Charts and graphs can also be used to represent geographic information. When you encounter these, you may need to draw on your knowledge of math. Look at this question:

3. Of the countries on the chart below, which one's population is growing the fastest?

Country	Population 1998	Population 2025 (est.)
	(in millions)	
Russia	147.2	131.4
United States	273.8	332.5
Zambia	8.7	16.1
Zimbabwe	11.9	19.3

Do not be fooled by the large numbers for the United States and Russia. In the Russian case, the population is expected to *decrease* over the time period. Remember, the second set of numbers are for a future date, so they are estimated (est.). For the United States, the increase by 2025 is large, but a rate of population increase is measured in percentages. The U.S. growth is not a high percentage of the total. Both Zambia and Zimbabwe are expected to grow more rapidly. Which is expected to grow faster? You will have to do the math to be certain. Zambia is expected to grow by 7.4 million people, an 85 percent increase over its 1998 population. Zimbabwe is expected to grow by 7.4 million people also, but this is only 62 percent of its 1998 population. This means that Zambia is expected to grow faster, based on current trends.

This information could also be shown on a map with the percentage of expected population increase marked inside each country, or it could be shown on a graph.

Key Questions for WHII.1 c–e

1. **How has geography influenced history?**
2. **Where are the world's major nations located?**
3. **What are some important trends in human migration and cultural interaction?**

1. GEOGRAPHY IN HISTORY

It is difficult to understand *what* happened in history without understanding *where* it happened. Places that are close together influence each other faster and more deeply than places that are far apart. Places that have valuable natural resources develop differently from places that are poor in resources. Location also influences the lifestyles and cultural characteristics of people.

Climate. One important way that location affects people's lives is through its influence on climate. Places in the low latitudes, close to the Equator, have hot climates. Some of these are damp, as in the tropical rain forests. Some are dry, as in the deserts. Places in the middle latitudes have more moderate climates. Finally, the arctic and subarctic regions in the high latitudes have extremely cold climates.

Wind patterns also influence climate. In South Asia and Southeast Asia, for example, the climate is dominated by the **monsoon** winds. These winds change direction according to the time of year. The southwest monsoon of May to October brings heavy rain. Because the monsoons provide water for agriculture, human life depends on their timely arrival. Farther east, out over the Pacific Ocean, violent interactions of wind and water produce **typhoons**. These severe storms frequently strike the Philippines, Japan, and other Pacific countries. The immense destructive force of these storms provides a challenge for architects and city planners in all of these countries.

Climates influence where people live, how they make their living, and often whether or not they are vulnerable to conquest by others. The fierce Russian winter helped to defeat invasions by Napoleon in the 19th century and Hitler in the 20th. Tropical weather and vegetation in Southeast Asia reduced the effectiveness of U.S. advanced weaponry in the Vietnam War. Bright, open desert locations made air power the key to victory in a series of Arab-Israeli conflicts and in the Gulf War against Saddam Hussein.

Natural resources. Economic development requires **natural resources**. Some natural resources are renewable, as in the case of soil, water, and forests. Others are nonrenewable, as in the case of fossil fuels (oil, coal, and natural gas) and minerals. Good farmland is one of the most valuable natural resources. To be profitable, however, farmland must be managed well. Good farmland in the Soviet Union could not save farmers from disaster when Stalin suddenly forced them onto huge, government-controlled collective farms.

Some countries do not have many natural resources. Japan is an example. How did Japan try to solve its natural resource problem in the 1930s and 1940s? In Chapters 10 and 11, you will read that Japan tried to conquer lands rich in the resources it lacks, especially petroleum (oil).

Japan attacked Pearl Harbor and went to war with the United States over these resources.

By the 1970s, oil was once again at the center of world history, as troops of the Soviet Union moved into Afghanistan and appeared ready to strike at the oil-rich Persian Gulf. U.S. President Jimmy Carter announced the "Carter Doctrine," which said that the United States would "use any means necessary, including force" to protect essential resources. Later U.S. presidents have put Carter's proclamation into action. A number of international affairs experts believe that conflicts over natural resources will dominate the 21st century.

2. MAJOR NATIONS OF THE WORLD

Physical size, population, economic strength, military power, available resources, and the presence or absence of major conflicts are some of the factors determining a country's role in the world. Do you know that the United States is the leading economic power in the world? Do you know that Germany and Japan made astonishing economic recoveries after World War II? Have you heard about the "ethnic cleansing" in Serbia and the genocide in Cambodia? How quickly can you find all of the numbered countries on the world outline map on page 8?

How did you do with these?

Now for some challenges. Here some more important countries. You will not need to know all of these countries to do well on the test, but the more countries that you identify, the more quickly and accurately you will be able to answer the questions. The simplified outline maps used in this section are standard features of the SOL test. Practicing with these maps will make the test easier.

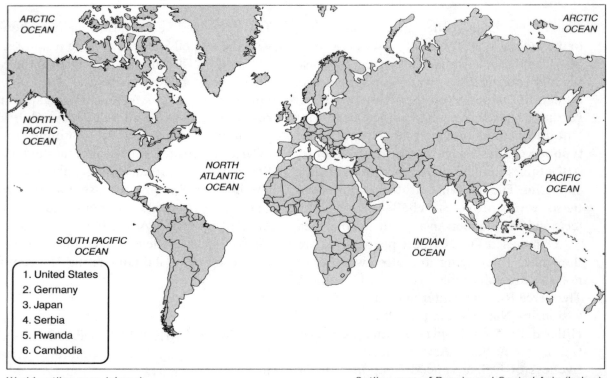

ARCTIC OCEAN

ARCTIC OCEAN

NORTH PACIFIC OCEAN

NORTH ATLANTIC OCEAN

PACIFIC OCEAN

SOUTH PACIFIC OCEAN

INDIAN OCEAN

1. United States
2. Germany
3. Japan
4. Serbia
5. Rwanda
6. Cambodia

World outline map (above).

Outline map of Russia and Central Asia (below).

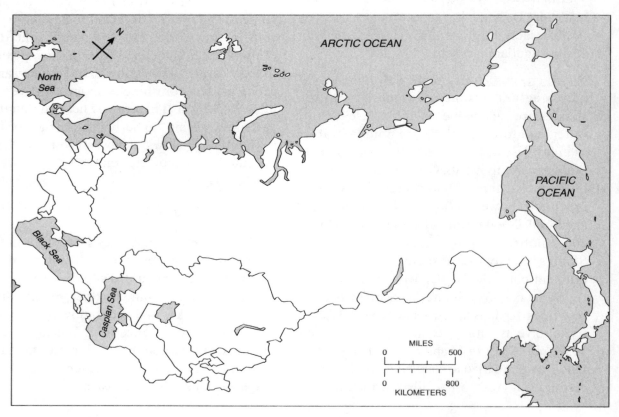

ARCTIC OCEAN

North Sea

PACIFIC OCEAN

Black Sea

Caspian Sea

MILES
0   500

0   800
KILOMETERS

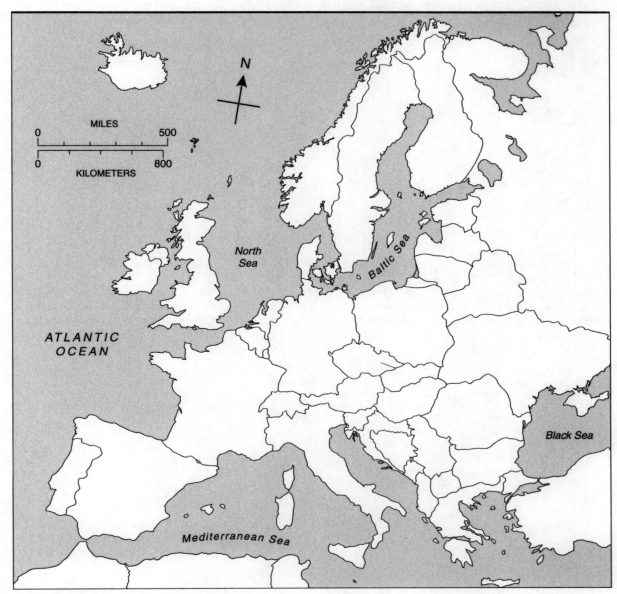

Outline map of Europe.

On the other map on page 8, locate Russia, Kazakhstan, and Turkmenistan.

On the map above, locate Switzerland, Luxembourg, Germany, the United Kingdom, Ukraine, Italy, France, and Spain.

On the top map on page 10, locate Kuwait,

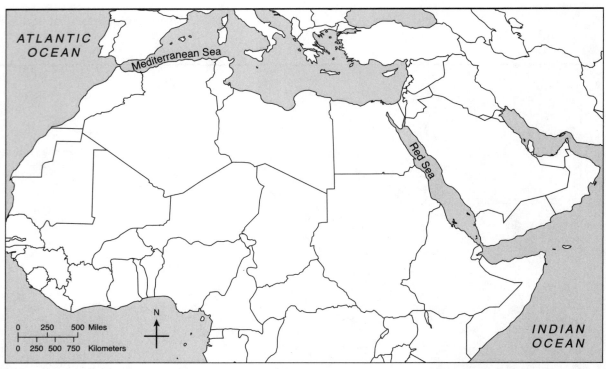

Outline map of the Middle East and North Africa (above).   Outline map of Sub-Saharan Africa (below).

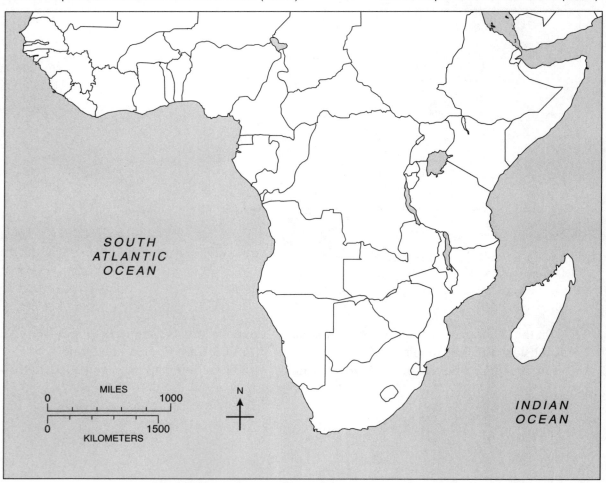

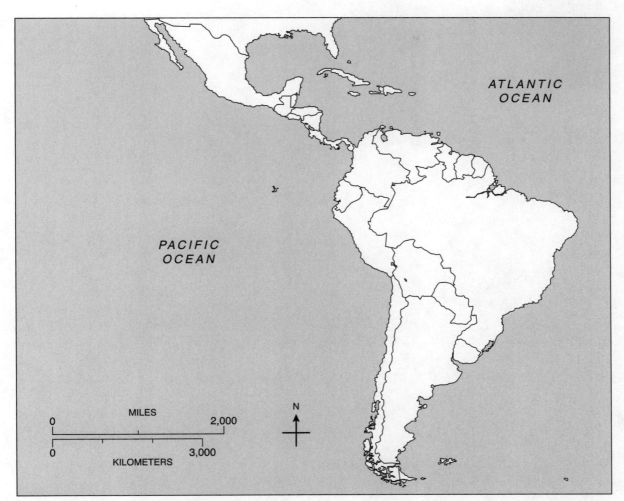

Outline map of Latin America and the Caribbean.

United Arab Emirates, Qatar, Israel, Algeria, Saudi Arabia, Libya, Iran, Turkey, Egypt, Syria, Jordan, and Lebanon.

On the bottom map on page 10, locate South Africa, Gabon, Botswana, Republic of the Congo, Sudan, Chad, Mozambique, and Madagascar.

On the map above, locate Mexico, Belize, Guatemala, El Salvador, Honduras, Nicaragua, Costa Rica, Panama, Colombia, Venezuela, Guyana, Surinam, French Guiana, Ecuador, Peru, Bolivia, Brazil, Paraguay, Argentina, Uruguay, Chile, Cuba, Haiti, Puerto Rico, Jamaica, and the Dominican Republic.

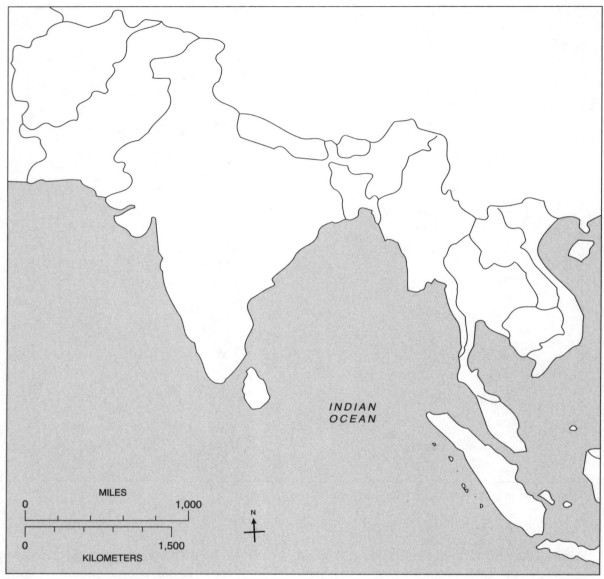

MILES

0   1,000

0   1,500

KILOMETERS

INDIAN
OCEAN

N

Outline map of South Asia.

On the map above, locate Afghanistan, Pakistan, India, Nepal, Bhutan, Bangladesh, and Sri Lanka.

On the map on page 13, locate Mongolia, China, Japan, Taiwan, the Philippines, Indonesia, Malaysia, Thailand, Cambodia, Burma, Laos, Vietnam, North Korea, and South Korea.

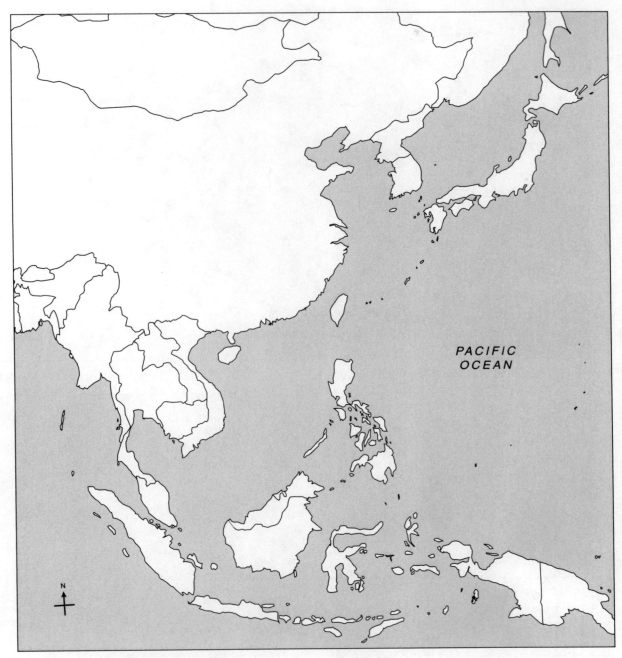

Outline map of East Asia and the Pacific.

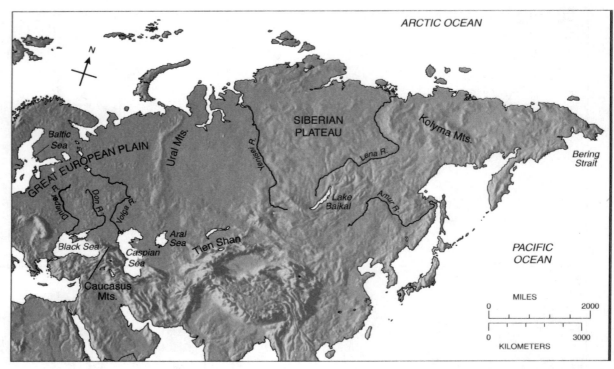

Physical map of Russia and Central Asia (above).

Physical map of Europe (below).

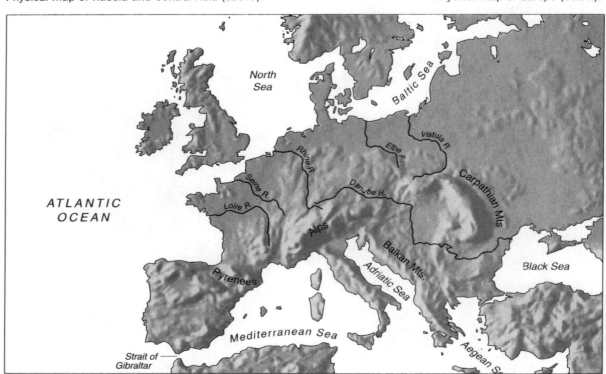

Locating physical features. Now locate the physical features that have influenced the history of the major regions of the world.

On the top map on page 14, locate Pacific Ocean, Arctic Ocean, Caspian Sea, Bering Strait, Lena River, Yenisei River, Amur River, Volga River, and Aral Sea.

Then locate Ural Mountains and Caucasus Mountains.

On the bottom map on page 14, locate Atlantic Ocean, North Sea, Mediterranean Sea, Aegean Sea, Adriatic Sea, Strait of Gibraltar, Rhine River, Seine River, Danube River, and Black Sea.

Then locate the Alps, the Pyrenees, and the Balkans.

On the map below, locate Atlantic Ocean, Pacific Ocean, Caribbean Sea, and Amazon River Basin.

Then locate Sierra Madre Mountains of Mexico, Brazilian Highlands, and Andes Mountains.

Physical map of Latin America and the Caribbean.

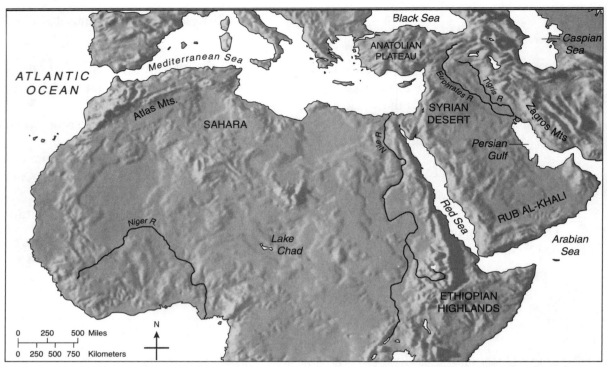

Physical map of the Middle East and North Africa (above).

Physical map of Sub-Saharan Africa (below).

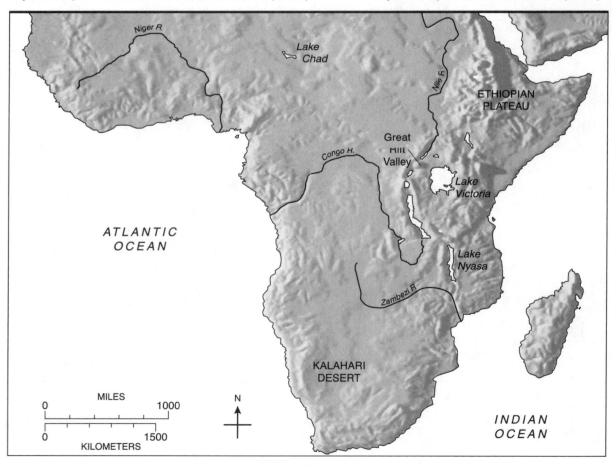

On the top map on page 16, locate Mediterranean Sea, Persian Gulf, Red Sea, Black Sea, Arabian Sea, Nile River, Tigris River, and Euphrates River.

Then locate Atlas Mountains, Anatolian Plateau, Sahara, and Zagros Mountains.

On the bottom map on page 16, locate Atlantic Ocean, Indian Ocean, Nile River, Zambezi River, Niger River, Congo River, and Lake Victoria.

Then locate Ethiopian Plateau and Great Rift Valley.

On the map below, locate Pacific Ocean, South China Sea, East China Sea, Sea of Japan, Yellow River (Hwang He), Yangtze River (Chang Jiang), and Mekong River.

Then locate Tien Shan Mountains and Tibetan Plateau.

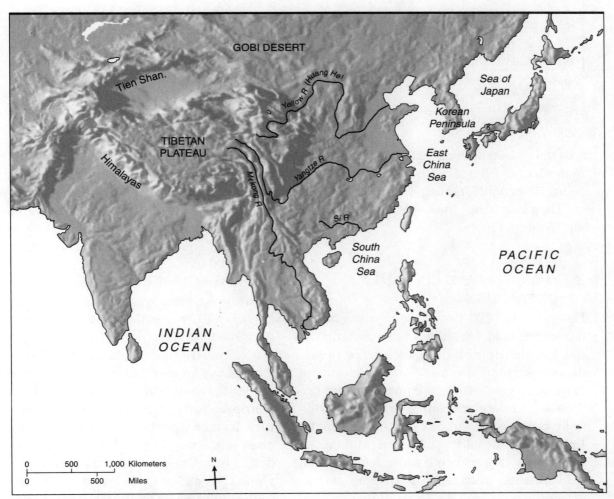

Physical map of East Asia and the Pacific World.

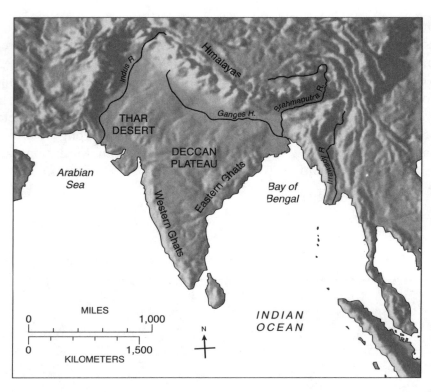

Physical map of South Asia.

On the map above, locate Arabian Sea, Indian Ocean, Bay of Bengal, Ganges River, Indus River, and Brahmaputra River.

Then locate the Himalayas and the Eastern and Western Ghats.

3. MIGRATION AND CULTURAL INTERACTION

Long before 1500, people were often on the move over land, sometimes as conquerors. As a result, the English of today are not the **indigenous** (there-from-the-start) people of England, today's Turks are not indigenous to Turkey, and even the Native Americans originally came to the Americas from elsewhere. Improved shipbuilding and navigational science in the 15th and 16th centuries, however, made possible even more massive migrations of people over long distances. Between 1500

and the present, millions of people have migrated (1) as chattel slaves, (2) as immigrants seeking a better life, and (3) as refugees of war and persecution. You can use this simplified formula to remember three of the important trends in migration and cultural interaction from 1500 to the present.

Between 1500, when Portuguese enslavement of Africans was in high gear, and the early 1800s, when the British government abolished the slave trade, 10 million or more Africans were transplanted to the Americas. Europeans immigrated to the Americas during that time also, but the greatest period of European immigration came in the 19th century. Rather than being forced, these European immigrants came freely in search of a better life that the Americas (primarily the United States, but Canada and Latin America too) were believed to offer. The third category of immigrants, refugees of war and persecution, dominated the 20th century. In one case, Nazi persecution and later genocide forced many Jews to flee Germany in the 1930s and 1940s. Revolutions, civil war, and abuses of human rights continued to create large numbers of refugees throughout the 20th century.

Wherever groups of people move, they bring their cultures with them. Geographic features often direct the patterns of human migration and therefore influence cultural interaction. For example, the mass transport of enslaved Africans to the Americas was related to the soil and climatic conditions that encouraged the plantation growing of cotton, sugar cane, and tobacco along the warmer eastern coasts of the Americas. Similarly, conditions perfect for growing wheat and corn in the North American "heartland" drew millions of willing immigrants in the 19th and 20th centuries.

Ideas can also flow from one culture to another without mass migration. The nearness of the Japanese islands to the cultural powerhouse of China facilitated the flow of Chinese ideas in their direction, although Japan's lack of farmland and other resources worked against Chinese migration there.

Small, navigable bodies of water have historically linked cultures, while mountains and larger bodies of water have isolated them. Before Columbus, the Atlantic Ocean kept American and European cultures separate from each other. Earlier still, Greek city-states only a few miles apart developed contrasting lifestyles—because those miles contained mountains.

From the perspective of the 21st century, **cultural diffusion** has overpowered geographic boundaries. Human curiosity, courage, greed, and technology have brought the world's cultures into contact. Modern world history is the attempt to understand how this happened.

SUMMING UP

History reveals the progress of people, places, and ideas over time. It sheds light on how we have gotten where we are. While history extends back in time, geography reaches out across space. It shows how people, places, and ideas compare around the world in our own time. Together, history and geography can help you answer many more questions than those raised in this book.

Chapter

2

The World in A.D. 1500

Virginia Standard of Learning WHII.2

The student will demonstrate an understanding of the political, cultural, and economic conditions in the world in about A.D. 1500 by

a. **locating major states and empires.**

b. **describing artistic, literary, and intellectual ideas of the Renaissance.**

c. **describing the distribution of major religions.**

d. **analyzing major trade patterns.**

e. **citing major technological and scientific exchanges in the Eastern Hemisphere.**

Standard WHII.2 a–e. The world in 1500

Setting the Scene

Though there is nothing magical about years with multiple zeroes in them, the year 1500 does, in some important ways, divide the medieval world from the modern world. Most importantly, it marks the beginning of true global interaction. Up to that time, merchants carried goods and ideas back and forth through Africa, Asia, and Europe, but the Americas were largely unknown to Europeans and Asians. After 1500, the empires of the Americas had highly eventful contacts with the empires and states of the Eastern Hemisphere.

Key Questions for Standard WHII.2 a–e

1. What were the major states and empires in the world in 1500 and where were they located?

2. How did the Renaissance revitalize Europe?

3. Where did the five major world religions play important roles in 1500?

4. What trade patterns and technological exchanges linked the states and empires of 1500?

1. STATES AND EMPIRES IN 1500

Western Europe was still primitive compared to the Chinese and Ottoman empires at the end of the 15th century, but several European nations rose in the 16th century to the level of important actors in the world. Even then, European states were relatively small. Ming China, the most advanced state of the time, had 100 million inhabitants, which was equal to all of Europe.

The major states and empires of 1500 are listed here. Can you locate them on the map below?

England	China (Ming Dynasty)
France	Japan
Spain	Mughal empire
Portugal	Songhai
Russia	Incan empire
Ottoman empire	Mayan empire
Persia (Safavid Dynasty)	Aztec empire

While this list includes the major *unified* states at 1500, two other locations were home to important developments of the period. The small Italian trading states enjoyed a new level of prosperity that triggered a cultural explosion. Meanwhile, the disunited **principalities** of the Holy Roman empire were soon to see religious conflict and reform within Christianity.

2. THE RENAISSANCE IN EUROPE

In 1500, Europe was in the midst of a cultural revival called the Renaissance. It was marked by excellence in art, literature, and philosophy. The word *Renaissance* means "rebirth," referring to a renewed emphasis on classical Greek and Roman ideas. One reason that the Renaissance is associated with the birth of the modern world is the humanist philosophy of the time. **Humanism** is a view of the world with human needs and hopes at the center. Renaissance humanism contrasted with the somber devotion of medieval Christianity. Renaissance artists like Leonardo da Vinci, Raphael, and Michelangelo portrayed humanity with a combination of powerful emotion and realistic detail. Petrarch and other writers explored

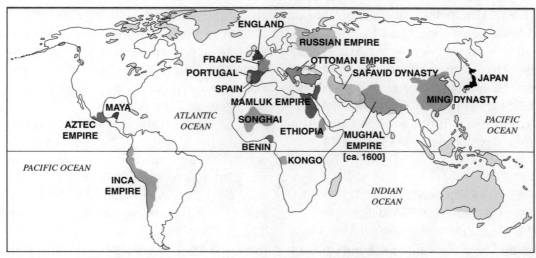

The world in A.D. 1500.

human emotions, especially love. By contrast, Niccolò Machiavelli in his how-to book for rulers, *The Prince*, focused instead on pointing out human strengths and weaknesses.

The Renaissance began in Italy and moved to Northern Europe. There it took on a new spirit, combining humanism with Christianity. It also spread widely among the common people through the use of the moveable-type printing press attributed to Johannes Gutenberg. The Northern Renaissance produced great literary works including Miguel de Cervantes's novel *Don Quixote* and the many plays of William Shakespeare. These works contributed to the rise of national pride in Western Europe.

3. INFLUENCE OF THE FIVE MAJOR RELIGIONS

In 1500, the five major world religions—Hinduism, Buddhism, Judaism, Islam, and Christianity—were influential in much of Asia, Europe, and Northern Africa. Islam was the most dynamic force in the world at this time, expanding in Europe, Asia, and northern Africa. Christianity and Judaism were concentrated in Europe and Southwest Asia (the Middle East). Hinduism was concentrated in India and Southeast Asia. Buddhism was concentrated in East and Southeast Asia. These religions were intertwined with governments of the time to varying degrees, with Islam and Christianity playing large legal and governmental roles. You will find more information about these developments in Chapter 14.

4. TRADE PATTERNS AND TECHNOLOGICAL EXCHANGES

By 1500, agricultural, technological, and scientific ideas had been exchanged among cultures in both the Western and Eastern Hemispheres. New trade patterns across the Atlantic Ocean began to connect with established Eurasian trade routes. Four of the most important of these established routes or networks were:

1. the Silk Road
2. the Indian Ocean trade network
3. the trans-Saharan caravan routes
4. the Mediterranean trade network.

Look for each on the map on the next page.

The Silk Road was an overland trade route that carried goods from the Mediterranean cultures across Mesopotamia, Persia, and Central Asia to China and back. This trade route was already in heavy use in 100 B.C., and it continued to carry significant trade until the 17th century.

The Indian Ocean trade network brought Chinese products by sea to destinations around the Indian Ocean and beyond. This trade linked the coastal lands of East Africa, southern Arabia, the Persian Gulf, India, Southeast Asia, and China.

The trans-Saharan caravan routes were responses to the challenges of the Sahara. At first, the routes played a small role in the exchange of products, but by A.D. 1000 large amounts of gold from the Niger River Basin were traded northward in exchange for salt from the Sahara. Other products, including kola nuts and palm oil, were traded northward from sub-Saharan Africa.

The Mediterranean trade network linked up with the Silk Road, the Indian Ocean network, and the trans-Saharan routes to distribute products to Mediterranean ports. In this way, Europe was connected to North Africa and to the Byzantine and Muslim empires. Through the Muslims and Byzantines, Europeans had contact farther east to China and

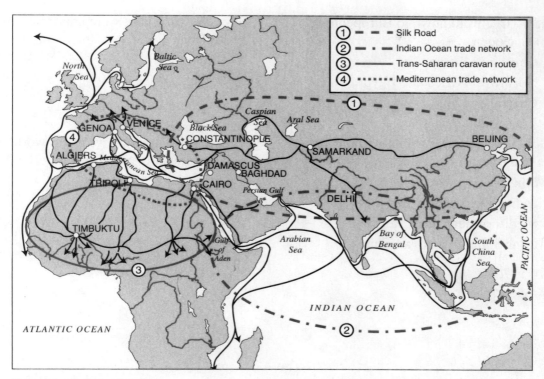

Four major trade routes.

India. Italian merchants dominated the profitable Mediterranean trade, and they played a large part in the European Renaissance described on the previous page.

Important items that were exchanged in this period included paper, the compass, silks, and porcelains (from China to Europe); textiles and spices (from India to Europe); gold and salt (in Africa); and sugar (from Southeast Asia to Europe and Africa). New ideas in medicine, astronomy, and mathematics (such as Arabic numerals) moved along the trade routes, primarily from urban centers in the Islamic empire to the trading ports of Western Europe.

SUMMING UP

As you learn more about modern world history, you will want to recall important starting points in culture, trade, and government from the years before 1500. By 1500, many of the fundamental features of the modern world were in place, including the five major world religions, early forms of modern nations, and extensive Eastern Hemisphere trade patterns that would become linked to the booming Atlantic trade of the 16th century.

CHAPTER REVIEW

1. Which of these states and empires occupied the largest area in 1500?
   a. Spain
   b. China
   c. India
   d. Songhai

2. Areas largely unknown to Europeans in 1500 included
   a. China and Korea.
   b. Northwest Africa and Egypt.
   c. Central and South America.
   d. India and Persia.

3. "Gold for salt" was a primary trading exchange on which route?
   a. Silk Road
   b. Indian Ocean trade network
   c. Mediterranean trade network
   d. trans-Saharan caravan routes

4. Silks and porcelains were important trade goods from
   a. China.
   b. Southeast Asia.
   c. Africa.
   d. Italy.

5. How many of today's five major world religions came into existence before 1500?
   a. 2
   b. 3
   c. 4
   d. 5

ERA

V

Emergence of a Global Age, A.D. 1500 to 1650

Chapter

The Reformation

Virginia Standard of Learning WHII.3

The student will demonstrate knowledge of the Reformation in terms of its impact on Western civilization by

a. **explaining the effects of the theological, political, and economic differences that emerged, including the views and actions of Martin Luther, John Calvin, and Henry VIII.**

b. **describing the impact of religious conflicts, including the Inquisition, on society and government actions.**

c. **describing changing cultural values, traditions, and philosophies, and assessing the role of the printing press.**

Standard WHII.3 a. Emerging differences: Luther, Calvin, Henry VIII

Setting the Scene

The Roman Catholic Church was a dominant force in Europe for centuries after the fall of the western Roman empire in A.D. 476. In the late medieval period, however, the Church was losing its power. Several factors contributed to the Church's declining influence:

- A great plague called the Black Death killed a third of the people of Europe between 1347 and 1350, including large numbers of the clergy. This catastrophe also undermined some Europeans' faith in the Church, which could not end the plague or even explain it.

- Because trade was increasing in Europe, merchants were becoming wealthier and more important. Their pursuit of wealth challenged the Church's teachings about greed. The Church's opposition to **usury** (the lending of money at interest) seemed especially out of touch with the lives of materialistic Europeans.

- Many Europeans began to think the Church was corrupt. When Catholics confessed their sins, the priest would set a **penance**, or a punishment, such as the saying of many prayers, for them to perform. Christians could be spared from a penance, however, if they purchased an **indulgence,** or a pardon. At first, indulgences only excused the buyers from their penance. Soon, however, priests eager to make money began telling people they could buy forgiveness from God and increase their chances of entering Heaven. The Church sometimes allowed men to buy their way into positions as priests. This unpopular practice was called **simony**.

- As nation-states became more powerful, people began to think of themselves as German, French, or Spanish instead of as simply Christian. Thus many Europeans outside of Italy began to resent the power that the pope in Rome held over their fellow citizens. Nobles in England and Germany were especially resentful of the pope's power.

Key Questions for Standard WHII.3 a

1. **How did the Reformation divide Europe between Catholics and Protestants?**
2. **What roles did Martin Luther, John Calvin, and Henry VIII play in defining Protestantism?**

1. EUROPE DIVIDED BETWEEN CATHOLICS AND PROTESTANTS

Simply put, Northern Europe became Protestant while Southern Europe remained Catholic. The Protestants took the revolutionary position that the Roman Catholic Church must be overthrown, while the Church took the extreme position that all **heretics** (people who did not accept a religion's teachings), should be destroyed. For more than a century, the people of Europe were forced to choose one side or the other. By the end of the 16th century, Europe was divided. By the end of the 17th century, Catholics and Protestants began to accept the fact that neither faith was going to disappear anytime soon.

2. MARTIN LUTHER, JOHN CALVIN, AND HENRY VIII

Martin Luther (1483–1546) and John Calvin (1509–1564) provided new views of faith and salvation, while English King Henry VIII excluded England from the pope's authority.

Martin Luther. Luther was a priest and a professor of theology (the study of religious thought). Beginning in 1517, he put forward three revolutionary ideas, which became the central belief of a form of Christianity called Lutheranism.

- *Salvation, or getting to Heaven, was won by a person's faith alone.* The Catholic Church taught that participation in the sacraments (the ceremonies of the Church) were necessary to gain entrance to Heaven. Luther disagreed, arguing that a Christian had only to believe in God. The sacraments, and even the priests themselves, were not necessary.
- *The Bible was the sole authority for Christians and should be available to everybody.* The Catholic Church insisted that only a priest could read and interpret the Bible. Luther's declaration that the Bible should become widely read and debated was a challenge to Church authority. In support of these ideas, Luther translated the Bible into German so that more people could read it. This further angered the leaders of the Church.
- *All faithful Christians were equal before God.* Since faith was all that mattered, all faithful Christians were equally righteous and equally guaranteed to enter heaven.

John Calvin. Calvin's approach to salvation differed from Luther's. He argued that humanity was divided in advance between the Damned (those who were going to Hell) and the Elect (those going to Heaven). God,

Martin Luther (1483–1546). Painting by Lucas Cranach (1472–1553).

Calvin said, already knew each person's fate. This view is called **predestination**.

According to Calvin, God had given the Elect a faith in Jesus Christ and a desire to live according to strict moral laws. Although no one knew whether he or she was going to Hell or going to Heaven, everyone who lived according to these strict laws could hope for Heaven. People should avoid worldly pleasures and always demonstrate moral virtues. The highest virtues for Calvin's followers were hard work, moral correctness, and thrift, or not spending money to show off. Calvinists believed that success in life showed God's favor. Scholars have called these ideas the "Protestant work ethic."

Henry VIII of England. This English king (reigned 1509–1547) played a double role in the Reformation. As Luther's beliefs spread across Europe, Henry VIII denounced him as a heretic. The pope was grateful for Henry's loyalty and named him "Defender of the Faith." Henry's loyalty did not last, however.

Henry wanted a male heir to his throne, but he was sure that his wife was growing too old to have a baby. He decided to divorce her so that he might marry a woman who could give him a son. Divorce was forbidden in the Catholic Church without special permission from the pope. When Henry asked for permission, the pope would not grant him a divorce. Henry reacted by calling a parliament of nobles and commoners to declare that the pope had no authority over the kingdom of England. Despite this action, the practices of the Church changed very little at that time. However, Henry's refusal to accept the domination of the pope started a process of change that resulted in the creation of the Church of England, or Anglican Church.

Standard WHII.3 b, c. Religious conflicts and changing cultural values

Setting the Scene

Although religious leaders such as Martin Luther and John Calvin began the Reformation, political leaders and rulers soon became involved. Protestantism offered relief from self-serving Church officials and oppressive Church practices. It also offered a chance to eliminate papal authority. Freedom from the pope's power made Protestantism more attractive to rulers.

Key Questions for Standard WHII.3 b, c

1. **How did religious conflicts influence European politics and economics?**

2. How were the new religious beliefs reflected in changing cultural values, traditions, and philosophies?

1. RELIGIOUS CONFLICTS

The Reformation produced dramatic changes across Northern Europe. New religious ideas spread quickly due to the printing press with movable type, which Johann Gutenberg put into common use in about 1450. Movable type printing had been invented in China much earlier, but it had immediate and dramatic practical success in Europe in the 1450s. The printing press promoted literacy and gave more people access to ideas.

The Reformation in Germany. Germany was the home of Martin Luther, and northern Germany became strongly Protestant. In this process, many north German princes increased their own power at the expense of the Catholic Church.

Not all Germans were ready to leave the Catholic Church, however. Many south German princes remained Catholic. Furthermore, most of Germany was officially part of the Holy Roman Empire, which was strongly Catholic. For many years, there was a tense peace between Catholics and Protestants in Germany and surrounding lands. Then in 1618, a long, violent war broke out between the Holy Roman Empire on one side and Protestant German principalities, together with such Protestant nations as Denmark and Sweden, on the other side. This war is known as the Thirty Years' War. Although the war started out as a religious conflict, over time certain politicians, including Cardinal Richelieu of France, made national power the war's main focus.

The Reformation in England. Henry VIII made himself the head of the Church in England. He seized Catholic Church lands and wealth. He closed the English monasteries. Yet he did not change the Catholic **liturgy** (form of service) or sacraments. Each of his three children ruled after him, and each was caught up in this complex religious situation. First, Edward VI increased the power of the Protestants. Then Mary restored the pope as head of the English Church. Finally, Elizabeth influenced Parliament to declare her the head of the Church of England. With this Act of Supremacy, a separate Anglican Church was created with the monarch at the head.

The Reformation in France. Calvinism spread quickly through France despite the monarch's opposition. The French Calvinists were called Huguenots (HEW-guh-nots). Many nobles be-

King Henry VIII (reigned 1509–1547).

came Huguenots, an action that was a matter of political as well as religious choice. Between 1562 and 1598, there were many conflicts between Huguenots and Catholics. The bloodiest of these events was the St. Bartholomew's Day Massacre, when some leading Catholics organized the murder of 10,000 Huguenots. Finally in 1589, a Huguenot noble called Henry of Navarre became King of France. To win the loyalty of his Catholic subjects, he converted to Catholicism, though he did not abandon his Huguenot allies. Henry's support of both Catholics and Huguenots produced a step toward religious tolerance in France. He issued a decree called the Edict of Nantes, which made Catholicism the nation's official religion but also let the Huguenots worship freely and participate in politics. Unfortunately for the Huguenots, the Edict was later revoked.

The Counter-Reformation. As Protestantism spread, popes and Catholic clergy members worked to reform the Catholic Church. They were motivated by a desire to eliminate corruption, but they also wanted to combat the popularity of Protestantism.

In the 1540s, the Catholic Church laid down several policies that countered the challenges of Martin Luther and other Protestants. The policies declared that:

- the Church, not the individual, interpreted the Bible.
- Church traditions had authority over the lives of Christians equal to the Bible's.
- faith alone was not enough to win salvation. A life of good works was necessary as well.

At the same time, Church leaders took firm steps to find and destroy heresy. A committee of six cardinals called the Inquisition was empowered to prosecute people for heresy and punish them by death. Begun as a method of reinforcing Church doctrine, the Inquisition became a terrifyingly unjust institution that relied on torture in its investigations and executed people by burning them at the stake, among other methods.

The Jesuits. The Catholic Church was aided in its mission to reform itself and fight Protestantism by the Society of Jesus, whose members were called Jesuits. The Jesuits believed in discipline and obedience to the pope. Many Jesuits traveled to distant parts of the world to convert people to Catholic Christianity. They carried the message of the Catholic Church as **missionaries**, and they improved the image of the clergy through their dedication to a pious life.

2. IMPACT OF THE NEW RELIGIOUS BELIEFS

Even before Martin Luther took his stand in opposition to the Church, reformers tried to infuse Church teachings with the humanist ideas of the Renaissance. Humanists believed in the ability of people to improve themselves through reason and logic. They valued the ideas of classical Greek writers, and they believed in the power of education. The most influential Christian humanist was Erasmus. His book *The Praise of Folly* criticized many aspects of society including the medieval practices and beliefs of the Church. Though Erasmus and the other humanists sought reform within the Church, their writings created an atmosphere for revolutionary changes.

From 1555 to 1690, continuous warfare over religion and national territory made kings cling to power and suppress their people. In some nations, however, new forces began opposing the power of kings. Commerce was

Queen Elizabeth I (reigned 1558–1603).

one of these forces. Through new commercial ventures, the middle class gained wealth, which the kings needed to support their armies. The kings could get this money through taxes only if they agreed to give up some of their power to the middle class. Thus, commerce was a force for democracy.

Some historians believe that the Reformation stimulated commerce by breaking down Church control over economic life. As commerce expanded, the role of merchants and financiers, called capitalists, increased. (This is discussed on page 33, "The Dutch Republic.")

England. As you read on page 29, Henry VIII's defiance of the pope led eventually to the establishment of the Anglican Church as the state Church of England. Over time, these actions redistributed both power and land. Henry passed out Catholic Church lands to loyal landowners who had pledged their support to the king and to the Anglican Church. As a result, the Anglican Church flourished. It later spread to the American colonies, where it broke with its English leadership during the American Revolution, forming the independent Episcopal Church.

In Ireland, however, which was then under English rule, the Church of England failed to gain popularity. The Irish held to their Catholic beliefs. Catholic priests led their parishioners in resisting Anglicanism. The Irish became increasingly resentful toward the English, while the English became increasingly intolerant of Irish beliefs.

Queen Elizabeth I. After the Catholic Queen Mary's death in 1558, Elizabeth came to power and reestablished the Anglican Church. She wanted to restore harmony in England, however, so she had Parliament pass a religious settlement aimed at reducing the conflict between Catholics and Anglicans. This settlement restored some of the Catholic liturgy to the Church of England. Throughout her reign (1558–1603), Elizabeth used her considerable political skill to lower tensions among the English people and strengthen the nation. As a result, England enjoyed prosperity and power, and religious controversies were safely managed until after Elizabeth's death.

King James. Queen Elizabeth died in 1603 and was succeeded by her cousin James I, who was already King of Scotland. (England and Scotland would formally join as Great Britain, or simply Britain, a century later.) James believed in the **divine right of kings**, meaning that a monarch's power is given by God and therefore the monarch can do whatever he or she pleases. James did not get along with England's Parliament, whose members did *not* agree that his right to govern came from God. They argued that he could not pass laws to tax the people without Parliament's consent. Nevertheless, James gave the people of England a gift when he ordered a new English translation of the Bible. This translation was called the King James Bible in his honor.

<u>The Dutch Republic</u>. The inhabitants of the northern part of the Netherlands were known as the Dutch. The Netherlands had been part of the Holy Roman Empire for centuries, and in the 16th century it was under the rule of Philip II of Spain. The Dutch were divided between Catholicism and Calvinism, but they were united by a desire to expel the Spanish from their lands. After years of desperate fighting, they won independence in 1581. The independent Dutch provinces shared three important characteristics:

- *Republicanism instead of monarchy.* The Dutch united their provinces into a republic, a country ruled by elected representatives of the people. The Netherlands royal family, the House of Orange, still played a part, however. The head of the family joined the group of governors that the Dutch chose to make important decisions. The new governors had to please the merchants and landholders of their provinces if they wanted to keep their positions.
- *Religious and intellectual freedom.* Unlike the other nations of Europe at the time, the Dutch accepted both Protestantism and Catholicism, and they even tolerated

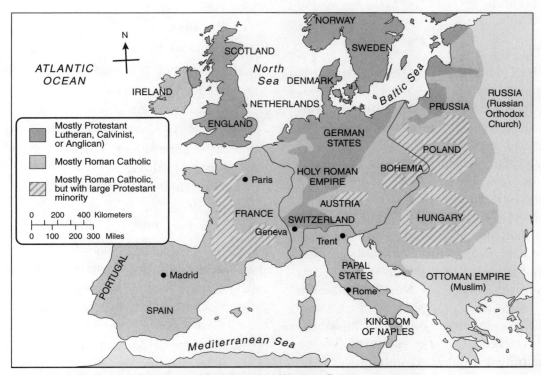

Major religions (Roman Catholic and Protestant) in Western Europe.

Jews, who were persecuted in almost every other nation in Europe. The Dutch were rewarded for their tolerance when foreign merchants and scholars of many faiths made Dutch provinces their homes.

- *Commercialism*. The Dutch were great merchants. They understood the principle of buying goods when and where they were cheap and selling them when and where they were expensive. The Dutch traded timber, food, spices, and other goods from all parts of the world then known to Europeans. To pay for the shipping of the goods, they offered shares of the potential profits to anyone who would contribute money. The money was called **capital**. The contributors were called **capitalists**. The hope of gaining rich returns on their **investments** encouraged many Dutch people to fund trading ventures.

SUMMING UP

The Catholic Church served the spiritual needs of Europeans for centuries with little competition from other systems of belief. In the Renaissance, however, a philosophy of human needs and values, called humanism, had spread northward and westward from Italy and found acceptance among the literate middle class. While the humanists criticized the Church in their writings, Luther, Calvin, and other reformers challenged the Church directly. They declared new ideas of faith and salvation. Political conflict followed, and Europe divided itself along religious lines. Northern Europe became Protestant (mostly Lutheran, Calvinist, or Anglican) while Southern Europe remained Catholic. At the same time, the Reformation strengthened state power over religious authorities, thus supporting the rise of

distinctive nation-states. In these ways, the Reformation helped to create modern Europe.

CHAPTER REVIEW

1. The changes known as the Reformation came because of
   a. the conflicts of the Thirty Years' War.
   b. concerns about the practices of the Catholic Church.
   c. the decline of the authority of the Holy Roman emperor.
   d. the increasing influence of Catholic missionaries in Eastern Europe.

2. The influential religious leader who introduced the concept of predestination and the avoidance of frivolous activities was
   a. Martin Luther.
   b. Henry VIII.
   c. Erasmus.
   d. John Calvin.

3. The Reformation came to England when
   a. Henry VIII became Defender of the Faith.
   b. Elizabeth I became Queen.
   c. King James I had the Bible translated into English.
   d. King Henry VIII divorced his wife.

4. One unexpected result of Luther's challenge to the Church was that
   a. English power increased.
   b. the Holy Roman emperor was able to defeat the Turks in Austria.
   c. North German princes increased their power.
   d. peasants in Germany and England demonstrated their loyalty to the Church and the Holy Roman Empire.

5. A significant result of the Reformation in Europe was that it
   a. strengthened state power over religious authorities.
   b. brought a long period of peace to Europe.
   c. forced Henry VIII of England to quit the throne.
   d. opened the way toward democratic practices in Europe.

6. It could be concluded from the map "Major Religions in Western Europe" on page 33 that
   a. the Catholic Church retained its greatest support in Northern Europe.
   b. Calvinist teachings made strong inroads in Spain.
   c. religion was a dividing factor in France.
   d. the Catholic Church lost influence in Italy.

7. Perhaps Martin Luther's greatest impact came when he
   a. supported the sale of indulgences.
   b. persuaded the pope to accept differences among Christians.
   c. translated the Bible from Latin into German.
   d. encouraged the German peasants to revolt against their princes.

8. The Reformation in Europe influenced American history because
   a. new religious ideas traveled to the American colonies.
   b. European nations wanted to expand the ideas of religious toleration.
   c. no Catholics settled in the English colonies.
   d. the Holy Roman Empire was losing influence and needed new areas in which to expand.

9. In the new commerce of the 16th century, traders offered shares of the potential profit in exchange for
   a. political support.
   b. supplies of manpower.
   c. religious freedom.
   d. investments of capital.

4

European Expansion Into the Americas, Africa, and Asia

Virginia Standard of Learning WHII.4

The student will demonstrate knowledge of the impact of the European Age of Discovery and expansion into the Americas, Africa, and Asia by

a. **explaining the roles of explorers and conquistadors.**

b. **describing the influence of religion.**

c. **explaining migration, settlement patterns, cultural diffusion, and social classes in the colonized areas.**

d. **defining the Columbian Exchange.**

e. **explaining the triangular trade.**

f. **describing the impact of precious metal exports from the Americas.**

Standard WHII.4 a, b. Explorers, conquistadors, and the influence of religion

Setting the Scene

In 1453, the Ottoman Turks seized Constantinople, the last stronghold of the Christian Byzantine empire. (Today it is the city of Istanbul, in Turkey.) The Muslim Ottomans thus gained a foothold in Europe and cut off many of the Europeans' trade routes with Asia. To satisfy their growing demand for trade, Europeans had to look for new routes. Prince Henry the Navigator of Portugal played a pioneering role by sponsoring voyages of exploration down the west coast of Africa, These voyages established trade routes that were later expanded around the tip of Africa and up the east coast to Asia. Portuguese explorations and those that followed by others were helped by technical improvements in shipbuilding and navigation, including a new kind of ship called the caravel, which was capable of making months-long ocean voyages. The caravel design grew with both Muslim and European technology, as did the compass and other new navigational devices. All of this brought about a new era of exploration and colonization of foreign territories. As European nations competed for new lands and trade routes, their efforts strengthened Europe's position in the world, often at the expense of other civilizations.

Key Questions for Standard WHII.4 a, b

1. **Who were the most influential European explorers of Asia, Africa, and the Americas?**

2. **Who were the conquistadors and what were their motives?**

1. INFLUENTIAL EUROPEAN EXPLORERS

Christopher Columbus, Vasco da Gama, Ferdinand Magellan, and Sir Francis Drake were important explorers from this time.

Christopher Columbus was an Italian sailor who convinced the King and Queen of Spain, Ferdinand and Isabella, to fund a voyage to Asia. Columbus thought he could sail west across the Atlantic Ocean and arrive in East Asia. In 1492, he actually landed on the islands known today as the Bahamas, Cuba, and Hispaniola. Because the Spanish monarchs had financed his journey, he claimed the lands he found for Spain. On his second voyage to the Caribbean, Columbus ordered the Native Americans he encountered to swear allegiance to the pope and to the rulers of Spain. Whenever Columbus encountered resistance from the Native Americans, he had his men murder them. As a result, Columbus has been both admired for his discoveries and condemned for his cruelties.

In the early 1400s, the Portuguese had already sent wave after wave of ships on voyages into the Atlantic Ocean and along the west coast of Africa. Their primary goal was to establish a sea route that would compete with the trans-Saharan caravan routes that dominated trade across North Africa and down the Red Sea into the Indian Ocean. Then in 1487, a Portuguese explorer named Bartolomeu Dias (bar-toh-loh-MEH-oo DEE-osh) rounded the Cape of Good Hope on the southern tip of Africa. Eleven years later, Vasco da Gama retraced the path of Dias, then went on across the Indian Ocean to a port on the coast of India. Da Gama's voyage established a Portuguese trade route to India.

Ferdinand Magellan was a Portuguese nobleman who believed he could sail around the Americas to Asia and come home by continuing around Africa. In 1519, he set out with five ships financed by Spain. Only one ship, with 18 men, survived the journey. Magellan did not make it; he was killed in the Philippines. The survivors, however, brought news that the Americas were vast and that the world was larger than most people had thought.

By 1577, the Spanish were well established in Central and South America (see the following section). An English captain named Sir Francis Drake then began attacking Spanish merchant vessels that were bringing goods back from their colonies. He waged a pirate war against the Spanish, stealing much Spanish gold for his Queen, Elizabeth I. The Spanish chased him part way around the world, and he decided to go all of the way around. Thus, he duplicated the achievement of Magellan's crew.

These early explorers were not able to finance their expeditions on their own. They were forced to look to government leaders for financial support. In exchange for this assistance, the explorer was obligated to claim any new land in the name of the sponsoring country. Columbus and Magellan both claimed lands for Spain. Drake claimed land for England. Soon, explorers sponsored by other countries would join the hunt for colonies.

2. THE CONQUISTADORS

Columbus explored all of the major islands of the Caribbean. The Spanish quickly learned that the inhabited region of the Americas also included vast lands to the west and south of the Caribbean, and they sent soldiers called

Key voyages of exploration: Columbus, Magellan, and Drake.

conquistadors (kon-KEES-tuh-dorz), or conquerors, to these places.

The conquistadors were motivated by three desires. They wanted to find gold and precious metals, convert the people living in the Americas to Christianity, and win fame for Spain by increasing its empire. Some people summarize these goals as "Gold, Glory, and God." The most successful of the conquistadors were Cortés and Pizarro.

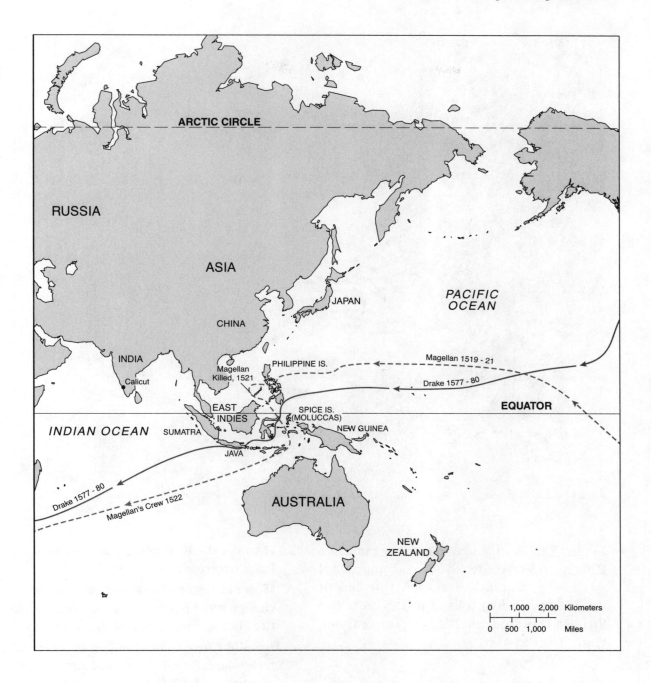

In 1519, Hernando Cortés began the conquest of Mexico. He had learned of a flourishing civilization called the Aztecs. He marched his 600 men through the mountains to the Aztec capital of Tenochtitlán (teh-noch-teet-LAHN).

He finally starved the city into submission with help from the bitter enemies of the Aztecs—the Tlaxcalans (tílas-KAH-lanz). (The Tlaxcalans say they succeeded with some help from the Spanish. It depends on who tells the story.)

Aztec emissaries making a treaty with the seated Cortés. His interpreter Malinche is shown standing to his left.

In the 1520s, Peru was conquered by Francisco Pizarro. Pizarro deceived and murdered Atahualpa (ah-tuh-WAHL-puh), the king of the Inca people who lived in the area. The Spanish captured and held the Inca capital, Cuzco (KOOS-koh).

Standard WHII.4 c–f. Colonial settlement and trade

Key Questions for Standard WHII.4 c–f

1. **How did the arrival of the Europeans affect the native peoples?**

2. **How did the Europeans maintain their lands overseas?**

3. **How did European expansion overseas change trade patterns and economic practices in Europe, Asia, and the Americas?**

4. **How did European expansion change the technologies, economies, and agricultural practices of both the colonies and their parent countries?**

1. EFFECTS ON THE NATIVE PEOPLES
Impact of European diseases. The most devastating effect of the Spanish conquests was the

importation of European diseases into the Americas. The Native American peoples had no immunity against European diseases such as swine flu, smallpox, and measles. Millions of people died as a result.

A new kind of slavery. As European tastes for American products increased, so did the need for laborers on plantations in the Americas. (**Plantations** are large farms on which most of the workers live.) Profit-hungry Europeans satisfied this need through slavery. They first attempted to enslave the Native Americans, then brought large numbers of enslaved Africans to the Americas.

Slavery had existed in Egypt, China, India, Greece, Rome, and other places, but the Europeans created a new kind of slavery that was race-based. Whereas in the past people had become slaves because of misfortunes such as being captured in wars or losing all their possessions, Africans were now assigned to slavery based solely on their dark skin. Also, the new slavery was **hereditary**, meaning that if you were born to slave parents you would be a slave too.

The two early slave-trading countries were Portugal and Spain. By 1690, however, the English also used the trade to provide workers for their plantations in the Caribbean. Later the English used the slave trade to provide labor for tobacco and cotton plantations in what became the Southern United States.

A new social class system. One lasting result of the Spanish colonies was the creation of a new social class system in Mexico and parts of Central and South America. Since the Spanish settlers were mostly men, over time there were many marriages with Native American women. The children of these marriages were called **mestizos** (mes-TEE-sohs)—mixed Spanish and Native American people. A hier-archy developed with the Spanish at the top, Native Americans at the bottom, and mestizos in between. The Spanish kept most of the wealth.

2. EUROPEANS AND THEIR LANDS OVERSEAS

The Europeans settled the areas where they traded and fortified them with military forces to defend them against other nations and local warriors. These settlements were called **colonies**. Colonies were trade centers as well as places where Europeans made native people accept Christianity and live by European laws. Europeans found that rice, tobacco, and cotton could be grown on plantations if there were enough laborers to do the work. There were not enough European laborers, so first Native Americans and then Africans were put to work on the plantations.

Where European nations settled colonies. Most of the land in the Americas was divided among the major European powers and remained under the control of these powers for centuries. The Spanish settled Central America, the west coast of South America, and much of western and southern North America. The Portuguese colonized the eastern part of South America, which now makes up the modern nation of Brazil. The English settled on the eastern coast of North America. The French settled north of the English, in what would become eastern Canada.

3. CHANGING TRADE PATTERNS

European nations sought wealth from their colonial possessions. According to mercantilism, the economic theory of the time, a nation's trade should be very heavy on exports (goods

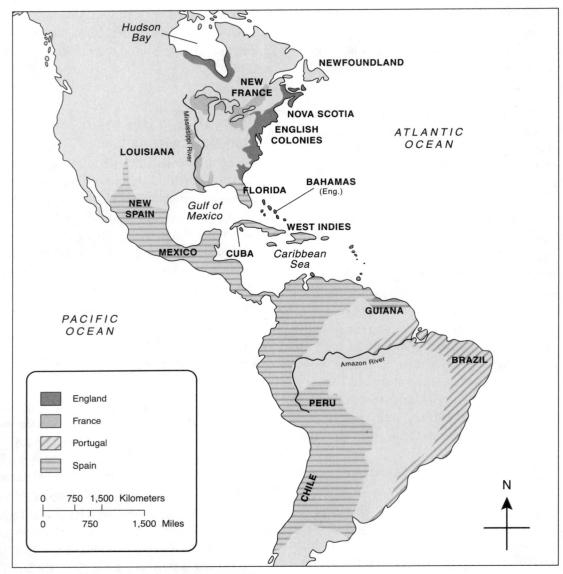

European land claims in the Americas in 1700.

sold to other countries). By exporting many goods and spending little on imports, the nation built up a store of wealth in silver and gold. If silver and gold could simply be taken from the colonies, that was good mercantilism too.

Soon after the establishment of armed trading posts in Africa and colonies in the Americas, a **triangular trade system** arose. Europeans sailed to Africa, where they sold European manufactured goods and guns to Africans in return for enslaved Africans. They then sailed across the Atlantic to the Americas, where plantation owners paid a high price for the Africans to use them as laborers. The traders purchased cotton, tobacco, and sugar from the Americas and took them back to Europe to sell.

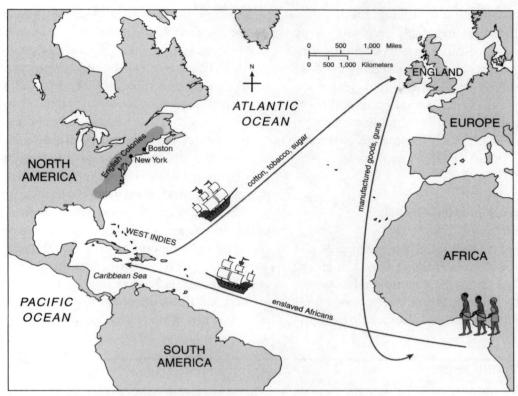

The triangular trade system during the 1700s.

The Spanish (and also the French in North America) were eager to convert Native Americans to Christianity. The Jesuits, as you learned in Chapter 3, were dedicated to conversion, and they traveled throughout the Spanish colonies. These missionaries were accompanied by soldiers. Spain not only wanted to save souls in the Americas, it also wanted to find and take as much gold and silver as possible back to Spain to pay for the Spanish monarchs' frequent wars.

The Spanish wanted to exploit their colonies for immediate gain. They supported farming that yielded valuable crops for trade, and they mined for gold and silver. They did not develop local industries.

The Spanish brought to their colonies the political idea of **absolute rule**—that is, rulers giving orders from the top down, with no questioning. The influence of this idea is one reason why Latin American nations would later have difficulty developing into democracies.

Protestant states such as England and the Netherlands also used a mixture of force and persuasion to promote their religion and their laws among native populations. These countries, though, were less concerned than the Spanish about saving souls. They were more interested in building colonies that were profitable.

Both the Dutch and especially the English brought democratic ideas to colonial governments. In particular, the rights of the individual against unfair imprisonment and taxation advanced significantly in England's American colonies. Such rights, however, applied only to the European settlers, not to Native Americans or enslaved Africans.

English colonial investments made many English merchants wealthy. By purchasing large English country estates, these merchants promoted themselves into the English upper social class. In a similar way, plantation owners in the American South gained social status and political influence from their profitable **cash crops**. Thus, powerful people on both sides of the Atlantic were linked to the colonial trade.

4. CHANGING TECHNOLOGIES AND ECONOMIES

Since many of the exchanges of goods, people, and ideas began with the explorations of Columbus, they are often called the **Columbian Exchange**. The exchange included trade goods, agricultural products and practices, and also human beings.

European expansion into the Americas meant the introduction of new goods on both sides of the Atlantic. The arrival of American goods in Europe strengthened the drive to establish and expand colonies. The first colonies in the Americas sent food products to Europe that most Europeans had never seen, such as corn, potatoes, and tobacco. As Europeans became more and more accustomed to these new items, the demand for them grew. This demand meant that more people were willing to pay high prices for the goods. Thus, traders and colonists, seeking profit, increased their colonies' farming efforts wherever they could.

In the Americas, European farming practices increased efficiency but destroyed native economies. The Europeans brought horses to the Americas, which had no native horses. The

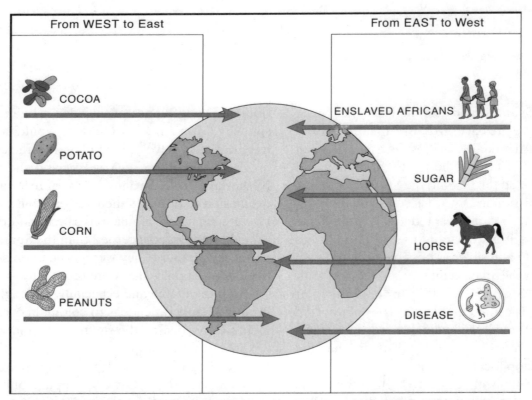

The Columbian Exchange included people, their cultures, technologies, and agricultural products. A few examples are shown above.

horses provided power for plowing and transporting crops, and European cattle provided a new food source. Horses also provided a means for managers of the plantations to check on workers throughout the large area of a plantation. As the plantation system took over, Native American farmers found themselves no longer free to grow crops in traditional ways, organized around the needs of their villages. The same happened in India and Africa, where Europeans also imposed their agricultural practices at the expense of the traditional economies.

The China trade. Silver from Spain's American colonies traveled a long way. It went first to Spain, where it was used to buy goods from other European countries. Its greatest impact, however, came at the heart of the world trade network, in China. While China produced a wealth of goods that Europeans wanted, particularly Chinese porcelains, European goods such as coarse woolens and mechanical clocks had only limited markets in China. Silver was the exception. In the late 1400s, China converted to a silver-based currency and demanded silver in payment for Chinese export products. Though trading silver to China was contrary to the theory of mercantilism, Europeans could not resist the appeal of Chinese porcelains, silks, and tea. American silver was the product that fueled Chinese trade with Europe from the 15th to the 19th centuries.

SUMMING UP

From the 16th to the 19th centuries, Europeans expanded into the Americas, Africa, and Asia. Massive cultural and economic exchanges took place. The profits of this new trade stimulated European expansion, as the European powers competed with one another for overseas lands.

European expansion brought both benefits and problems to the native peoples. One deadly exchange was the importation of European diseases into the Americas, wiping out the Native American populations. The transatlantic slave trade that provided laborers for plantations was inhuman. European domination of African, Asian, and American lands disrupted native cultures and economies.

CHAPTER REVIEW

1. One factor that aided the Spanish conquest in the Americas was that
   a. the Native Americans eagerly converted to Christianity.
   b. millions of native inhabitants died of diseases spread by the Europeans.
   c. the Spanish soldiers usually outnumbered the native inhabitants.
   d. there were no cities that the Spanish had to conquer.

2. Use of enslaved Africans as workers in the Americas was supported by all of the following factors except
   a. an established slave trade in Africa.
   b. the spread of labor-intensive plantations.
   c. a strong European desire for American agricultural products.
   d. a high percentage of women among Spanish settlers.

3. A long-term effect of the Spanish conquest was
   a. a social hierarchy that put the native inhabitants at the bottom.
   b. the earliest beginnings of political democracy in the Americas.
   c. Spanish control of Brazil.
   d. protection of the religious and social customs of the native inhabitants.

4. An important effect of the Spanish conquest in the Americas on Europe was
   a. an increase in European exploration of the Americas.
   b. a decrease in the authority of the Church.
   c. a lack of interest in developing the African slave trade.
   d. a decrease in competition among European nations.

5. The drawing of an early encounter between Cortés and the Aztecs on page 40 best indicates that
   a. the Aztecs were afraid of Cortés.
   b. a fight was beginning to develop.
   c. the meeting seemed to be friendly.
   d. the Aztecs seemed afraid of Cortés's horse.

6. The three points of the triangular trade show on page 43 were
   a. Europe, Australia, and the Americas.
   b. Asia, Europe and the Americas.
   c. Asia, Africa, and the Americas.
   d. Europe, Africa, and the Americas.

7. Which colonial power was most committed to "absolute rule" in the Americas?
   a. England
   b. the Netherlands
   c. Spain
   d. Portugal

8. The nation whose products had such appeal to Europeans that they traded silver for them was
   a. China.
   b. India.
   c. Cuba.
   d. the Philippines.

Chapter 5

Global Trade and Regional Civilizations

Virginia Standard of Learning WHII.5
The student will demonstrate knowledge of the status and impact of global trade on regional civilizations of the world after A.D. 1500 by

a. describing the location and development of the Ottoman empire.

b. describing India, including the Mughal empire and coastal trade.

c. describing East Asia, including China and the Japanese shogunate.

d. describing Africa and its increasing involvement in global trade.

e. describing the growth of European nations, including the Commercial Revolution and mercantilism.

Standard WHII.5 a.
The Ottoman empire

Setting the Scene

From ancient times, networks of trade routes linked Africans, Europeans, and Asians and provided pathways for the flow of ideas and goods. From a world perspective, however, the impact of this trade was limited. The civilizations of the Western Hemisphere remained isolated, and even along the central routes of the Eastern Hemisphere most of the goods passed only into the houses of the wealthy. After 1500, European exploration and expansion created new and more influential links among the world's civilizations.

Key Questions for Standard WHII.5 a

1. **How did the Ottoman Turks create a powerful empire?**

2. **What part did the Ottomans play in world trade?**

1. HOW THE OTTOMANS CREATED THEIR EMPIRE

The Ottomans were followers of a Turkish leader named Osman. Their rise was linked to the decline of the Byzantine empire, which in the 12th century suffered many setbacks, including attacks by the Seljuks, Turkish nomads who migrated westward from east of the Aral Sea around the Caspian Sea to Anatolia (the Asian part of today's Turkey). Even more serious than conflict with the Seljuks was an attack on Constantinople by knights from the Fourth Crusade. The knights captured and plundered the city in 1204. Though the Byzantines recaptured their capital in 1261, their empire was badly weakened.

Meanwhile, starting from a small principality on the Black Sea, the Ottomans steadily expanded. By the end of the 14th century, they had taken Macedonia, Serbia, and Bulgaria from the Byzantines. Then the Ottomans were themselves overrun and defeated by invading Mongols led by Timur the Lame. Mongol rule was brief, however. The Ottomans recovered quickly after Timur's death in 1405.

By 1453, the Ottoman Sultan, Mehmed II, was ready to lay siege to Constantinople. His cannons smashed holes in the city's walls, and his soldiers stormed the city, bringing the Byzantine empire to an end. The Ottomans renamed the city Istanbul, from the Greek *is tin poli* meaning "to the city."

In 1517, the Ottomans conquered Egypt and Syria. This made the Red Sea the Ottomans' southern frontier. To further strength their position, the Ottomans invited the rulers of the port cities of Algiers and Tunis to join the empire voluntarily. After this, the Ottoman navy was able to challenge the European

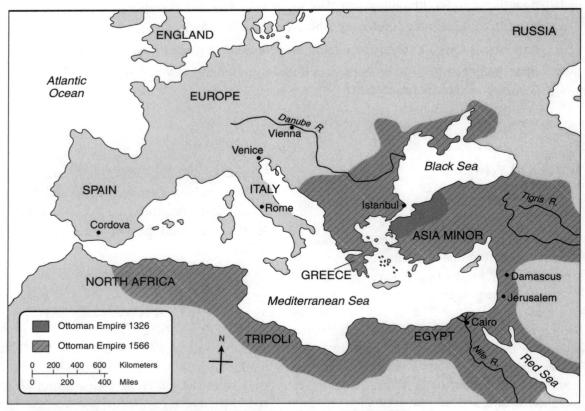

The Ottoman empire, from first lands held (1326) to expansion (1520–1566).

fleets throughout the Mediterranean Sea, and Ottoman merchants expanded their already large trading network in which coffee and ceramics were important products. As the Ottomans expanded into Europe, they came into conflict with the Holy Roman Empire. Through a series of military victories, the Ottomans occupied the Balkans, and over time, many people there converted to Islam.

The reign of Suleiman the Magnificent (from 1520 to 1566) was the greatest period of Ottoman power. Suleiman modernized the Ottoman army, which went on to defeat the Hungarians and came close to capturing Vienna (then in the Holy Roman Empire, today in Austria). Suleiman established a sound administrative system and a legal system that lasted into the 19th century. The security and organization that Suleiman gave the Ottoman empire contributed to its "golden age" of architecture, painting, poetry, and calligraphy, and in his time the Ottomans were the unquestioned leaders of the Muslim world.

2. THE OTTOMANS AND WORLD TRADE

By the middle of the 16th century, the Ottomans controlled the major trade routes between Asia and Europe. They ruled the lands from the Persian Gulf across Turkey and Greece into Hungary and across North Africa from Egypt to Algiers. Ottoman strength contributed to trade, since roads were safe and travel easy within the empire. Important Ottoman exports included coffee and ceramics.

Fighting between the Ottomans and Christians sometimes slowed but never stopped the Mediterranean trade. European goods and Spanish-American silver flowed from Tripoli through the Ottoman empire to Asia in caravans (long lines of camels). The caravans brought Asian goods back to the Mediter-

ranean ports for export to Europe. This process continued until the mid-17th century.

Standard WHII.5 b, c. India and East Asia

Setting the Scene

China in 1500 was the largest nation in the world. It dominated the East Asian world in a way that no nation could dominate Europe. China's influence had gone up and down over the years, but Chinese leaders maintained a steady confidence in their superiority to all outsiders. China was far superior to Europe in both economic power and in technology during the 14th and 15th centuries. In the 16th century, the positions reversed, and historians still debate the reasons for this.

Like the Chinese, the Japanese were also building a national identity. In Japan, power was distributed under a system of government called the shogunate. In northern India, meanwhile, Mongol rulers called the Mughals maintained an uneasy rule.

Key Questions for Standard WHII.5 b, c

1. **Who were the Mughals and how did they establish an Indian empire with a profitable coastal trade?**

2. **How did the Chinese and Japanese attempt to limit the influence of European merchants?**

1. THE MUGHALS AND THEIR INDIAN EMPIRE

Descendants of the Mongols, the Muslim Mughal rulers established an empire in northern India in the early 16th century. India is far from the homeland of Islam, and Mughal rule was never popular in Hindu India, so the Mughal leaders had to be effective military

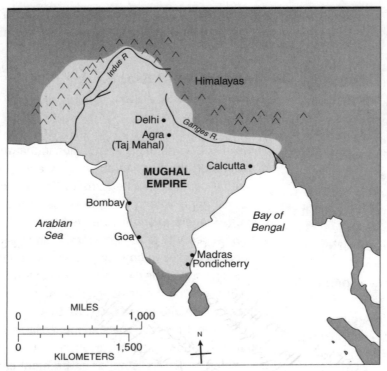

Mughal empire in India.

leaders. Akbar, who ruled from 1556 to 1605, was also a brilliant organizer. He divided the empire into provinces run by trained administrators. He promoted religious toleration, improved the tax system, and made use of Hindus as administrators and army commanders.

The religious toleration promoted by Akbar was short-lived, but Islamic cultural influences have lasted to the present day. One of the Mughal rulers built the famous Taj Mahal as a mausoleum (elaborate tomb) for his favorite wife. The Taj Mahal is one of the world's most beautiful buildings, blending Islamic and Indian artistic themes.

Perhaps the greatest success of the Mughal rulers was strengthening the Indian economy. Under their rule, Indian agriculture produced a variety of cash crops (sugar, opium, tobacco, and others) in addition to staple food crops. In-dian industry produced high-quality textiles and iron products, including cannons. Indian coastal trade continued to be highly profitable even after 1500, when the Portuguese (followed by the English, Dutch, and French) began building trading outposts along India's coast-line to compete for the Indian trade. Indian textiles played a large part in the English trade and influenced the developing English textile industry. The Mughal talent for enterprise is remembered in the English word mogul, which refers to a highly successful businessperson.

2. CHINESE AND JAPANESE RESTRIC-TIONS ON EUROPEAN MERCHANTS

Japan of the 16th century was a feudal society run by knights called **samurai**. In this respect, it was not so different from Western Europe. The

Japanese emperor had little power. This leading noble, called the **shogun**, ruled through military strength provided by his bands of samurai.

In the 1500s, the shoguns welcomed foreign traders and missionaries, but in 1622 the shogun began persecuting Christians. Japanese leaders feared the influence of foreign ideas and practices on their country. Foreign Christians were expelled, and Japanese citizens were forbidden to travel to other countries. European merchants were excluded from the country, except for a small group of Dutch merchants who had been careful not to promote European ways or Christianity to the Japanese. These Dutch merchants

were allowed to operate only from one island in Nagasaki Bay. A small group of Chinese merchants were also allowed to trade with Japan.

In the early 1500s, Portuguese merchants traded with the Chinese from the port of Canton, but they upset the Chinese people and their Ming rulers with their violent and undisciplined behavior. Wanting to gain the benefits of foreign trade without having to deal much with the European "devils," as the Chinese called them, the emperor limited the Portuguese to trading only out of a station at Macao. The Chinese adopted a policy of isolation against foreign influences despite strong

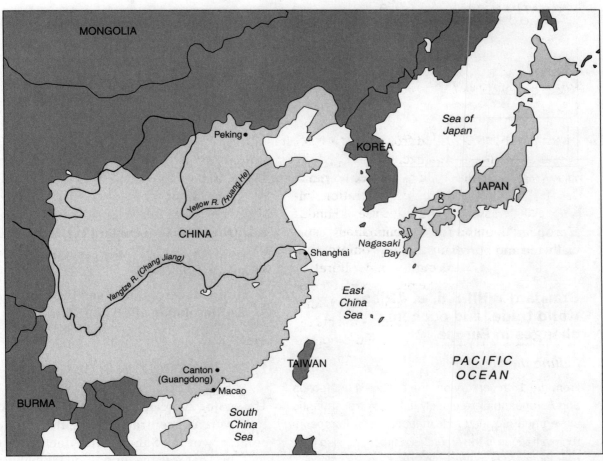

East Asia in the 17th century.

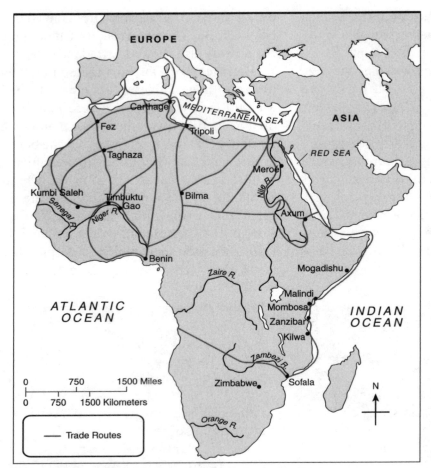

African trade routes and European trade forts, 1100–1500.

European demand for Chinese goods, especially tea and porcelains.

Standard WHII.5 d, e. Africa, world trade, and economic changes in Europe

Setting the Scene

From the 16th century on, the destinies of Africans and Europeans were closely linked. A transatlantic slave trade provided African laborers for European-run plantations in the Americas. Europeans also took over large areas in Africa and ran them as colonies.

<u>Key Questions for Standard WHII.5 d, e</u>

1. **How did Africa's role in global trade change after 1500?**

2. **How did mercantilism and the Commercial Revolution affect global trade?**

1. AFRICA'S ROLE IN GLOBAL TRADE AFTER 1500

The major African trading empires of A.D. 1500 were concentrated along the southern boundary of the Sahara, with one major exception. That was the empire of Zimbabwe in southeastern Africa. Africa played a central role in the Mediterranean trade network, trans-Saharan trade network, and Indian Ocean trade network. Numerous East African cities, notably Sofala, Zanzibar, and Mogadishu, were extremely prosperous as a result of the Indian Ocean trade.

After 1500, the slave trade increasingly dominated Africa's trading relationships. European plantations in the Americas needed laborers, who were supplied through the triangular trade involving Europe, Africa, and the Americas. First, Europeans traded their goods for captured Africans. Then in the "middle passage" or middle step in the process, the captured Africans were shipped to the Americas. In the final stage, sugar and other American products were carried back to Europe. From the late 1500s to the end of the 1700s, the number of Africans sent to the Americas was about 60,000 a year.

On the African coast, European trading forts protected the merchants, especially the slave traders. Few of the forts were ever used for fighting, since the African leaders benefited from the trade too.

During this period, enslaved Africans and agricultural raw materials streamed out of Africa, while manufactured goods from Europe, Asia, and the Americas, along with new food products (such as corn and peanuts), flowed into Africa.

2. MERCANTILISM AND THE COMMERCIAL REVOLUTION

Mercantilism. As European states expanded, they soon began to compete with one another for resources and wealth. European leaders followed a commonly held economic theory of the time called **mercantilism**. Under mercantilism, governments believed that the key to

maintaining the power of a state was to increase its supplies of gold and silver. Thus, the Spanish imported huge amounts of silver from their American colonies. The increased supply of silver boosted European trade, as the Spanish used it to purchase a wide range of goods, especially military supplies.

A second way for European countries to pursue their mercantilist goals was to grow valuable cash crops in the colonies. For example, English colonists grew tobacco and cotton where the climate was suitable. These crops brought a great deal of wealth to the home country. However, since mercantilism was designed to benefit the Europeans at the expense of the colonies, conflicts between colonies and their home countries were inevitable.

The Commercial Revolution. At first, monarchs had paid for voyages of explorations and the settling of colonies. As more and more colonies succeeded in providing gold or profitable goods for sale, private individuals became involved in the funding of colonies.

The Dutch pioneered the method of raising capital for trading voyages by promising investors a share of the profit. The individual capitalists combined their money, which made expensive ventures possible. They also shared the risks, which were too great for a single businessperson to accept. These **joint-stock companies** soon were funding most of the voyages of discovery and colonization. One such company sent the settlers who founded Jamestown, England's first permanent colony in North America, in 1607.

The English led the revolution in other business practices. The efficiency of the English trading companies made them the model for all European nations. These trading companies were supported by strong banking and insurance companies centered in London. By taking out insurance on their cargo ships, companies could carry out several risky voyages at one time. As time went on, English merchants also benefited from rapidly advancing technology, including improved shipbuilding techniques, and from the backing of the powerful English navy.

One further English success was the development of markets for English goods within the American colonies. The colonies became places to sell items, not only to make them. Efforts at this time to establish markets in India and China were, however, unsuccessful. These highly developed civilizations resisted European products in the 17th and early 18th centuries.

SUMMING UP

Between 1500 and 1700, Asian, African, European, and American cultures came together through exploration, conquest, and trade. In this process, the once backward nations of Western Europe used new technologies, business practices, and ideas of government to their own best advantage.

CHAPTER REVIEW

1. Which statement best describes the relationship between the Ottoman and Byzantine empires?
   a. The Byzantines and Ottomans rose and fell together as a result of their geographic settings.
   b. The decline of the Byzantines helped the rise of the Ottomans.
   c. The Ottomans and Byzantines were united against Western European rulers.
   d. The Byzantines and Ottomans were united by their common Islamic heritage.

2. In the 14th century, the Ottomans were overrun by the
   a. Mughals.
   b. Crusaders.
   c. Hungarians.
   d. Mongols.

3. The most important strategic location controlled by the Ottomans was the
   a. Black Sea.
   b. Aral Sea.
   c. Mediterranean Sea.
   d. Red Sea.

4. Mughal rulers in India belonged to what religious tradition?
   a. Hinduism
   b. Buddhism
   c. Islam
   d. Christianity

5. After expelling other foreigners, the Japanese allowed Dutch merchants to trade in Nagasaki Bay because
   a. the Dutch were too powerful to be stopped.
   b. Dutch merchants did not promote Christianity or European ways.
   c. Dutch products were more appealing than those of other nations.
   d. the Chinese had a special regard for the culture of the Netherlands.

6. The first Europeans to raise money for trading voyages by promising investors a share of the profits were from
   a. England.
   b. the Netherlands.
   c. Spain.
   d. Italy.

7. One reason for English trade success in the 17th and early 18th centuries was the
   a. worldwide use of the English language.
   b. failure of Spanish colonization efforts in America.
   c. efficient business practices of the English trading companies.
   d. high demand for coconut and cocoa, over which the English had a monopoly.

ERA VI

Age of Revolution, A.D. 1650 to 1914

Chapter

6

Absolutism, Enlightenment, and Reason

Virginia Standard of Learning WHII.6

The student will demonstrate knowledge of scientific, political, economic, and religious changes from about the 16th to 18th centuries by

a. **describing the Scientific Revolution and its effects.**

b. **describing the Age of Absolutism, including the monarchies of Louis XIV, Frederick the Great, and Peter the Great.**

c. **assessing the impacts of the English Civil War and the Glorious Revolution on democracy.**

d. **explaining the political, religious, and social ideas of the Enlightenment and the ways in which they influenced the founders of the United States.**

e. **describing the French Revolution.**

f. **identifying the impact of the American and French revolutions on Latin America.**

g. **describing the expansion of the arts, philosophy, literature, and new technology.**

Standard WHII.6 a. The Scientific Revolution and its effects

Setting the Scene

The world we live in today was shaped in large part by dramatic changes in Europe during the 16th, 17th, and 18th centuries. As you read on, you will learn how the terms absolutism, enlightenment, and reason fit those periods. Those three trends were involved in the most startling of all the changes—the Scientific Revolution.

To explain the nature of the world, most Europeans of the 16th century used only what they could directly observe. For example, they saw no signs that the earth was moving, so they felt certain that it was at rest. All of the stars and planets seemed to circle around the earth, so the earth was thought to be at the center of the universe. The idea of the earth at the center of the universe fitted well with Christian religious views of the times, which emphasized the special place of human beings in God's universe.

Such beliefs, which seemed common sense, were challenged during the Scientific Revolution. The leading scientists of ancient times had attempted to use everyday observations and logical reasoning to explain how the world worked. The new scientific theories were based on more thorough observations and record keeping, and, most importantly, on **experimentation** to test ideas. When scientists like Galileo and Isaac Newton found that their experiments and observations contradicted the accepted laws of the universe, they made the revolutionary argument that those laws would have to change.

Key Questions for WHII.6 a

1. **How did Copernicus, Kepler, Galileo, and Newton contribute to the new scientific theories?**
2. **How did the new science challenge established ideas and authority?**

1. COPERNICUS, KEPLER, GALLILEO, HARVEY, AND NEWTON

To explain the world and the universe, Copernicus, Galileo, Kepler, and Newton used observation and experimentation to explain the world and the universe. They founded the modern sciences of astronomy and physics. Harvey extended the use of new scientific principles to the study of the human body.

Copernicus moved the sun to the center of the solar system. The accepted model of the solar system had been put forward by an ancient astronomer named Ptolemy (TOL-uh-mee), who placed the earth in the center of the universe. Polish astronomer Nicholas Copernicus (1473–1543) challenged this model, arguing that the earth was a planet that revolved around the sun. Copernicus's model for the solar system is called the **heliocentric** (hee-lee-

oh-SEN-trik) system. He supported his claim with mathematical calculations about the orbits of the planets.

Unfortunately for Copernicus, his work was flawed in its observations and its assumptions. His observations of the movements of the planets were not accurate enough to support his mathematical calculations. Also, he assumed (wrongly) that the planets traveled in circular orbits. As a result, the Ptolemaic system could explain Copernicus's calculations equally as well as a heliocentric system.

Later discoveries, however, firmly demonstrated that the earth and the other planets orbit the sun. Danish astronomer Tycho Brahe (TEE-koh BRAH-hee, 1546–1601) made very extensive and accurate observations that more strongly supported Copernicus. Moreover, German astronomer Johannes Kepler (1571–1630) solved the problem of the planets' orbits. Nevertheless, Copernicus is credited with helping start the Scientific Revolution by providing the first new view of the universe in almost 2,000 years.

Kepler proved that the sun was the center of the solar system. Johannes Kepler discovered that the planets travel in stretched-out circles called **ellipses**, which cause each planet to be closer to the sun at one part of its journey and much farther from the sun at another part. Kepler developed three laws of planetary motion that, combined with Tycho Brahe's detailed observations of the planets' movements, made it possible to prove that Copernicus was right about the heliocentric solar system.

Galileo used a telescope to discover universal physical laws. The new science was bolstered by the use of instruments that made scientific observation more accurate than ever before. Using a telescope that he made himself, the Italian astronomer Galileo Galilei (1564–1642)

The Copernican (heliocentric) system of the universe with the sun (not the earth) as the center of the universe.

showed that the sun was not a perfect form, as Aristotle had written. Instead, it had dark patches called sunspots. He showed that the moon was not perfect either, but covered with mountains and craters. He even measured the mountains and found the highest ones to be 4 miles high, an estimate that scientists still consider accurate.

Galileo also used his telescope to discover the largest moons of Jupiter, which he sketched as they revolved around the planet. He supported Copernicus's theory that the earth was a planet orbiting the sun. He wrote his findings in a book called *Starry Messenger*. As you will learn in the next section, this small book and his later writings created serious problems for Galileo.

Galileo was a pioneering experimenter. He constructed careful and often elaborate experiments to test his theories. One of his most famous experiments demonstrated that heavy objects are not pulled to the earth any faster than lighter ones are. His findings challenged people to accept new ideas about the world, even when they contradicted what people already believed.

<u>Harvey described the circulation of blood in humans and animals</u>. English doctor William Harvey (1578–1657) published a study that showed how blood circulates through the body and explained how the valves of the heart function.

<u>Newton discovered the laws of gravity</u>. English physicist Sir Isaac Newton (1642–1727) proposed that there was a force, gravity, that attracted all objects to one another. Gravity, he argued, made things fall to earth, and it also made the planets revolve around the sun. The same force was at work on earth and in the universe.

In his book *Principia Mathematica* (Principles of Mathematics), Newton laid down three laws of motion that could predict the orbits of the planets or the movements of billiard balls on a pool table. Like gravitation, his laws of motion were universal. They were at work on earth and among the stars. The laws of motion solved a wide range of problems in science and engineering. Until 20th-century scientists such as Albert Einstein brought further innovations, Newton's laws formed the backbone of physics.

2. HOW THE NEW SCIENCE CHALLENGED AUTHORITY

The new science challenged the authority of the Church and the state by proposing that truth could be found only in observation and experimentation. Both Catholic and Protestant leaders interpreted Galileo's support of the Copernican theory of the heliocentric system as dangerous to Christian authority. By moving the sun to the center of the solar system,

Galileo and others relegated the earth to the role of orbiting planet. This made it hard to argue that human beings were the center of the universe. The pope ordered Galileo to stand trial for **heresy**. Under threat of torture and possible death, Galileo made a confession that the ideas of Copernicus were false. He was forced to live under house arrest until his death.

Galileo's experience shows how the established authorities in Europe perceived a dangerous challenge in the new science. The new theories suggested that truth could be found not in the teaching of the Church or the laws of the government, but only in observation and experimentation. From the time of Copernicus and Galileo, modern science has presented human beings with difficult ideas and has provoked religious debates that continue to the present day.

Standard WHII.6 b.
The Age of Absolutism

Setting the Scene

An **absolute monarchy** was a government in which one person had total or near total control of the financial resources and the laws of a country.

Monarchies had existed for thousands of years, and in some places the kings or queens had nearly total power, as in the Egypt of the pharaohs. In Europe during the Middle Ages, however, a king or queen's power over the people was limited. Under the feudal system, Europe was divided into many small kingdoms, and monarchs had to share their power with numerous nobles who ruled over their own estates. The Roman Catholic Church was the only centralized power, ruling over Western Europe with an extensive **bureaucracy**.

By the end of the Middle Ages, however, monarchs were beginning to gain power. This increasing royal power played a double role. On the one hand, it held back the trend toward individual rights and widespread participation in government that we call democracy. On the other hand, it enabled the absolute rulers to take steps their countries needed, like modernizing their economies.

To demonstrate the characteristics of absolute monarchies and the role they played in shaping European history, Standard WHII.6 b examines the reigns of Louis XIV (in France), Frederick the Great (in Prussia), and Peter the Great (in Russia).

Key Questions for WHII.6 b

1. **What factors contributed to the rise of absolute monarchies in Europe?**
2. **How did Louis XIV, Frederick the Great, and Peter the Great establish their absolute monarchies?**

1. THE RISE OF ABSOLUTE MONARCHIES

Between 1500 and 1800 in Europe, feudalism declined, cities grew, the middle class sought peaceful conditions for trade, and colonies provided wealth. All of these factors helped to strengthen the monarchs.

- The decline of feudalism decreased the local nobility's control over the land.
- Cities concentrated people and money together, where the monarch could control them more easily than when they were spread across the countryside.
- The middle class and the rise of trade provided an incentive for rulers to establish law and order across their kingdoms. More trade meant more wealth for the king to tax, and it was far easier to raise taxes when the kingdom was orderly.
- Monarchs could also pay for overseas colonies and reap the direct benefits of those colonies.

But even though the monarchs gained in power throughout this period, they could not make their rule absolute without overcoming the resistance of the nobility, the Church, and the rival monarchs of neighboring kingdoms.

2. THE ABSOLUTE MONARCHIES OF LOUIS XIV, FREDERICK THE GREAT, AND PETER THE GREAT

These three rulers are the prime examples of absolute monarchs. Louis XIV ruled France from 1643 to 1715. Frederick the Great ruled Prussia from 1740 to 1786. Peter the Great ruled Russia from 1682 to 1725. Each of them reigned during part of the 18th century, which was the height of the Age of Absolutism.

<u>Louis XIV</u>. Though Louis XIV was king of France from the age of nine, he did not rule

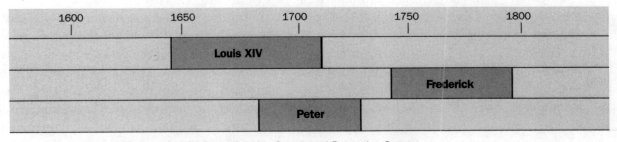

Three absolute monarchs: Louis XIV, Frederick the Great, and Peter the Great.

The colonnade around the courtyard of the Palace of Versailles, France.

alone until the death of his powerful chief minister, Jules Mazarin (ZHOOL mah-zah-RANG), when Louis was 22. At that point, Louis announced that Mazarin would not be replaced, that he would rule alone without a minister. He declared that he was subject to no one, and that his power came directly from God.

Louis based his rule not just on military power, but on financial and commercial control of France. He looked upon France's wealth as his wealth, and he sought to make his kingdom and himself as rich as possible. This was in keeping with Louis XIV's motto: "I am the state." He set up councils to over-

see the economy of his kingdom, to maximize the taxes and tariffs paid to him. One particularly able council secretary, Jean-Baptiste Colbert (kol-BEHR), raised huge revenues for Louis's monarchy.

Louis gained control over the nobility by bringing them all to his grand palace in Versailles, which he had built as a symbol of royal power. There, while they competed with one another for the favor of the king, Louis watched and judged their every action. He also appointed **commoners**—people who were not born to the nobility—into positions in his government. He knew he could trust the commoners to be loyal to him because they were grateful for their government positions.

Louis used his great wealth to maintain an army of 300,000 men, an extraordinary number for the time. He fought wars against Austria, the Dutch Republic, Portugal, the German and Italian states, and England, always trying to improve France's landholdings and wealth. Louis's aggressive policies united the French in the early years of his rule, but they eventually led to disaster. His costly and unsuccessful wars left France nearly bankrupt.

Frederick the Great. Frederick II was a well-educated Prussian. As a boy he had a passion for music, philosophy, and poetry. His father, however, frowned on his intellectual interests and forced him to live by military discipline. Frederick's father believed that military strength was the only way that Prussia would flourish, and he wanted to impose his belief on Frederick.

Frederick learned this lesson well. During his reign as the King of Prussia, he waged two great wars against neighboring Austria in order to expand Prussia's land holdings. During the Seven Years' War (1756–1763), Frederick, with only the British as his allies, successfully fought the powerful armies of France, Austria, Sweden, Saxony, and Russia. His army prevailed because it was the best equipped and best trained in Europe. Frederick often led it personally. He was a master of surprise attacks, and many of his victories were won because he caught his enemy unawares. His military genius ultimately earned him the title "the Great."

Although he sought to increase Prussia's power through war, Frederick also devoted his intellectual abilities to softening and improving the tough laws his father had given to Prussia. He championed greater religious tolerance, especially toward Catholics, who had been persecuted in Protestant Prussia. He also opened schools for the common people and schools to train government officials.

Peter the Great. Peter I is most remembered for his Westernization of Russia. While he was the Tsar of Russia, he visited the Netherlands, England, and Austria. After he returned, he tried to make Russia more like these Western European nations by changing its laws, its government, its military, and the social habits of its people. He made these changes by force.

He overcame the Russian nobility by promoting commoners to positions of authority and by earning their gratitude and loyalty in return. He also had to contend with the powerful Russian Orthodox Church. He triumphed by replacing its head, the patriarch, with a group of church leaders who reported directly to him.

Like Louis and Frederick, Peter the Great sought to increase the power of his country through warfare. He modernized the Russian army with up-to-date weapons, strategies, and training practices. He oversaw the creation of the Russian navy, which played a key part in his wars against neighboring rivals, Turkey and Sweden. Between 1700 and 1721, he fought Sweden, which was then one of the greatest powers in Europe. When Russia finally prevailed, it took Sweden's place on the European stage. Russia would be a major power in Europe from then on.

Peter moved Russia closer to Europe socially. He built a new capital on the Baltic Sea and named it St. Petersburg after his patron saint. The new capital was more accessible to European trade and ideas than Moscow. He also forced upper-class Russians to wear Western clothing and improve table manners while eating.

Expansion of Russian power and territory continued under Catherine II (Catherine the Great), whose long rule started in 1762. At first, Catherine seemed to be a more moderate ruler. She tried consulting with her subjects through a Legislative **Commission** to get its members' views of reform. Later, though, she shut down the Commission and ruled with absolute power.

Standard WHII.6 c, d. England's revolutions, Enlightenment ideas, and their influence on America

Setting the Scene

Nearly every revolution involves some kind of violence. England's Glorious Revolution, in which Parliament stood firm against an **authoritarian** king, was an exception. Back in 1641, however, a similar clash had led to a violent revolution—the English Civil War—that Parliament had won.

Key Questions for WHII.6 c, d

1. **What were the English Civil War and the Glorious Revolution?**

2. **What political changes were supported by these revolutions?**

3. **What Enlightenment ideas fueled these revolutions?**

4. **How did Enlightenment ideas influence the founders of the United States?**

1. THE ENGLISH CIVIL WAR AND THE GLORIOUS REVOLUTION

The English Civil War of 1642 to 1649. James I (reigned 1603–1625) and Charles I (reigned 1625–1649) attempted to rule as absolute monarchs. They challenged the ideas of limited government, such as one's right to jury trial and the power of Parliament to set taxes, which were taking hold in England. As a result, a civil war broke out between Charles I's supporters and supporters of Parliament. The revolutionaries finally executed Charles I and set up a republic led by Oliver Cromwell, who was called the "Lord Protector." The republic lasted until 1660, when the monarchy was restored.

The Glorious Revolution. This was the bloodless transfer of power from King James II to King William and Queen Mary in 1688. In 1685, James had become King of England, and he quickly angered and alienated his fellow citizens. He appointed Catholics to high offices, which was against a law that had been passed by Parliament. He dissolved the Parliament and never called it into session again. He gave every indication that he believed in the divine right of kings.

James II was a Catholic king in a strongly Protestant country. His second wife, who was Catholic, gave birth to a son, and it looked as

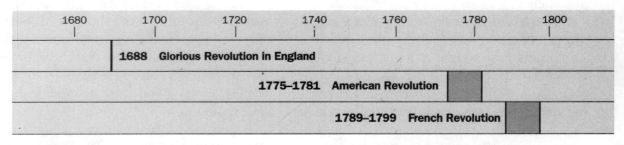

A century of revolutions: England's Glorious Revolution, American Revolution, French Revolution.

William III and Mary II ruled England jointly from 1689 to 1694, when Queen Mary died. Thereafter, King William ruled alone until his death in 1702.

though England would continue to be ruled by Catholic kings. James stationed 10,000 troops outside London. The king seemed to be leading England into another civil war.

Instead of a war, however, some English leaders turned to Mary, James's Protestant daughter from his first marriage. They invited her and her husband, William of Orange (the Dutch king), to accept the throne of England. As William's army arrived in England in 1688, James fled to France instead of fighting. The English called the overthrow of James II the "Glorious Revolution" because no one was killed.

In 1689, William became King William III of England, and Mary, the Queen. They signed a **Bill of Rights**, which limited the power of the monarch and established the permanent power of Parliament. England was declared a constitutional and Protestant state.

2. POLITICAL CHANGES SUPPORTED BY THE ENGLISH REVOLUTIONS

The English in the late 1600s were out of step with Europe's trend toward absolutism. The Glorious Revolution of 1688 in England moved considerable power from the monarch to Parliament. Gone were the beliefs in the divine right of monarchs and passive obedience to the government. After 1688, no English monarch could rule without the consent of Parliament. Thus, as a result of the English Civil War and the Glorious Revolution, parliamentary power became greater than royal power in England.

The English monarch's powers were limited both by the rise of Parliament and by traditional guarantees of the people's rights. These included **habeas corpus** (HAY-bee-us KOR-pus), the right of people to be safe from unfair imprisonment, and the right to a trial by jury. The limiting of the monarch's powers is sometimes called the rise of **constitutional monarchy**.

3. ENLIGHTENMENT IDEAS

The Age of Reason was a time when philosophers applied precise scientific thought to the problems of government and human relations. Its final phase, called the Enlightenment, was marked by highly creative and thought-provoking criticism of Western Europe's ideas and practices. In their emphasis on reason over religious doctrine, Enlightenment thinkers laid the foundation for the attitude of religious tolerance that played a major role in the American colonies.

4. ENLIGHTENMENT IDEAS AND THE FOUNDERS OF THE UNITED STATES

The Enlightenment spread from Europe to the American colonies in the 1700s through newspaper articles reprinted from Great Britain. Increased newspaper sales reflected the spread of literacy in the colonies, partly as a result of the Puritan emphasis on reading the Bible. Thoughtful Americans applied Enlightenment ideas of natural and political science to the problems that interested them.

John Locke's writings were especially influential in the American colonies. His ideas

Enlightenment Ideas That Provoked Revolutionary Actions

Name	Important work	Important ideas about what a government should be and do
Thomas Hobbes (England)	*Leviathan*, 1651	People are naturally wicked and need a strong government. Hobbes supported absolute authority, but he argued that power came from the need to manage people's behavior, not from divine sources.
John Locke (England)	*Two Treatises of Government*, 1690	Life, liberty, and property are natural rights, and government exists to protect those rights. When government fails to do so, the people have the right to change it.
Charles-Louis de Montesquieu (France)	*The Spirit of the Laws*, 1748	The government should be separated into different branches to prevent any one branch from gaining too much power. These branches should be the executive, the legislative and the judicial.
Jean-Jacques Rousseau (France)	*The Social Contract*, 1762	People are naturally good, but society corrupts them. In setting up a government, people choose to give up their self-interest for the common good. Government comes from the consent of the governed.
Thomas Jefferson	*The Declaration of Independence*, 1776	All men have certain inalienable rights, and when the government abuses these rights, the people have the right to overthrow the government.

were familiar to the writers of the Declaration of Independence and the writers of the Constitution of the United States. Locke drew many of his ideas from the writings of notable religious scholars. Unlike Thomas Hobbes, Locke felt that humans in the state of nature were reasonable and that certain rights belonged to people as their birthright. It was to ensure these rights, Locke said, that governments were created. Thus, government was a mutual obligation of those governing and those governed. If the former failed their obligations, the people had the right to resist.

Locke interpreted the Glorious Revolution in England as an example of the right to resist. In the Declaration of Independence, Thomas Jefferson interpreted the American colonists' dissatisfaction with Britain as an example of this right. The U.S. Constitution represented the social contract as the basis of government.

Standard WHII.6 e, f. The French Revolution; revolutionary ideas in Latin America

Setting the Scene

Unlike England's Glorious Revolution, France's Revolution of 1789 was an explosion of pent-up anger. Over decade after decade, French kings had made far too few changes in the face of the terrible suffering of the poor and the new political ideas sweeping Europe. Louis XIV (1643–1715) had held absolute power. In the first part of Louis XIV's reign, the way the French government ruled was considered an **enlightened despotism**. This meant that Louis attempted to put his power to useful purposes—centralizing the government, encouraging trade, strengthening the army, and enlarging the nation. The later years of Louis XIV's reign, however, showed more despotism and less enlightenment. Louis was constantly fighting expensive wars that caused his people great suffering.

In 1789, the government of France under Louis XVI was still based on old ideas from the Middle Ages. The people were divided into three **estates** (classes), and there were great differences among them:

- First Estate—clergy
- Second Estate—nobility
- Third Estate—a combination of the middle class, the city poor, and country peasants. The Third Estate made up about 98 percent of the French population.

Inequality was a major cause of the French Revolution. The First and Second Estates each had special privileges. The clergy controlled between 5 and 10 percent of French land, and much of the profit from this land went to high Church officials. The Church was not taxed, though it made "free gifts" to the king. The nobility was exempt from the most important tax, called the **taille** (TIE-y). Even within the Third Estate, wealth was wildly unequal: The rising merchant class, the **bourgeoisie** (boor-zhwah-ZEE) or middle class, was prospering, while the peasants and the urban poor saw very little improvement in their lives.

Key Questions for WHII.6 e, f

1. **What were the most important events of the French Revolution?**
2. **How did the American and French Revolutions affect Latin America?**

1. THE FRENCH REVOLUTION

The immediate cause of the revolution was a financial crisis. War debts were one problem, especially the high cost of helping the American colonies fight their American Revolution. The bad harvest year of 1788—another problem—resulted in a shortage of bread, which led to a rise in prices so that poor people could not afford bread. Many endured hunger and the possibility of starvation.

On July 14, 1789, revolutionaries captured the Bastille in Paris, a prison and a symbol of the French monarchy.

These are the main twists and turns of the French Revolution:

1. In May 1789, the nobles forced King Louis XVI to call for the Estates General to meet. This legislative body, made up of representatives of the three estates, had not met for more than 150 years. Meetings of the Estates General only succeeded in worsening the class conflicts. Members of the Third Estate withdrew and formed a National Assembly.

2. Workers and merchants in Paris in July armed themselves and stormed the Bastille prison, murdering government officials.

3. Peasant revolts broke out across France. The peasants burned nobles' manor houses and destroyed grain and tax records so they would not have to pay taxes.

4. The National Assembly issued the "Declaration of the Rights of Man" and wrote a constitution.

5. In 1792, a crowd mostly composed of women forced Louis XVI from his palace at Versailles to Paris, where he could be watched. That same year, the French government declared war on Austria, hoping to unite the French people by attacking another monar-

chy. As the war dragged on, violence broke out again within France. A new and more radical government, the National Convention, executed Louis XVI as a traitor, then set up a Committee of Public Safety to weed out enemies of the revolution. Thousands were condemned as enemies and guillotined during this period called the Terror. Even Robespierre (roh-besp-YEHR), the leader of the National Convention, was guillotined. His execution brought a strong reaction. The Terror ended, and a French Republic called the Directory was established in 1795.

6. In 1799, as problems plagued the Directory, a general named Napoleon Bonaparte launched a *coup d'état* (KOO deh-TAH, seizure of power by force) and took over the government.

The outcome of the French Revolution was a military dictatorship. Napoleon went to war against Britain, Austria, Russia, and Prussia and established an empire across Europe.

2. EFFECTS ON LATIN AMERICA

The American and French Revolutions were fueled by Enlightenment ideas about the rights of people, and they spread those ideas (see the table on page 68). Though the excessive violence of the later phases of the French Revolution disturbed many people, the idea of throwing off a repressive government spread to Latin America.

In the 1790s, enslaved Africans in Haiti (then called Saint-Domingue) revolted against their French colonial government. Napoleon was not able to defeat the revolutionaries led by Toussaint L'Ouverture, and since he could not regain Haiti, the emperor sold all of the French Louisiana Territory to the United States in 1803. This enabled Napoleon to withdraw his troops from Louisiana for use in Europe.

After Napoleon conquered Spain in 1808, revolutions broke out in the Spanish colonies. One of the revolutionary leaders, Simón Bolívar (boh-LEE-var), studied Enlightenment ideas of government in the United States (1807) and in London (1810). After a long independence struggle against Spain, Bolívar organized the Republic of Venezuela and also wrote the constitution of Bolivia. Independence came to much of Latin America, but the region suffered continuing conflict and disunity.

Standard WHII.6 g.
The arts, philosophy, literature, and technology

Setting the Scene

During the 17th and 18th centuries, great technological advances in Europe helped pave the way for the Industrial Revolution (discussed in Chapter 8). These advances included all-weather roads that

Simón Bolívar (1783–1830).

improved transport and trade, better farm tools that increased productivity, and improvements in shipbuilding that lowered shipping times and costs. New technologies not only transformed Europe economically, socially, and politically but also gave Europe an economic, cultural, and political influence over the rest of the world. It persists to this day.

The Enlightenment brought creative energy to the arts and sciences. Composers, artists, philosophers, and scientists all wrestled with the challenge of showing the proper relationship between the new ideas generated by reason and traditional Christian religious beliefs.

Key Questions for WHII.6 g

1. **What changes took place in music, art, and philosophy during the 16th, 17th, and 18th centuries in Europe?**
2. **How did European arts and sciences reflect Enlightenment ideas?**

1.   MUSIC, ART, AND PHILOSOPHY

Music. Composers developed increasingly complex works through what is called the **Baroque period**, a trend that reached its height in the early 18th century with the works of Johann Sebastian Bach. During the **Classical period** that followed, Franz Joseph Haydn (HY-dun) and Wolfgang Amadeus Mozart developed such balanced forms of music as the sonata and the symphony, which are still used today. There were technical improvements, too. The 18th century brought new or improved instruments, for example the piano and the clarinet, and somewhat larger and more diverse orchestras.

Until the 18th century, nearly all composers earned a living by writing music either for a church or for a wealthy patron such as a prince. Then public concert halls came into existence, and the idea of paying to hear music

began to spread among well-to-do members of the middle class. Among the rural working class, folk music continued to flourish as it had for centuries.

Art. Painters began to stress light and color and demonstrated new subtleties of shading. The English painter John Constable (1776–1837) and the French painter Eugéne Delacroix (duh-lah-KRWAH, 1798–1863) urged artists to be more imaginative and more sensitive to the moods of nature. They broke from the traditions of classical art and paved the way for the late-19th-century Impressionists (painters who focused even more closely on the surface effect of different lighting conditions).

Philosophy. In philosophy, one of the important Enlightenment ideas was **rationalism**. This was a view of the world that emphasized reason over faith. One of the most important rationalists was Voltaire (1694–1778), who wrote more than 100 volumes advocating tolerance, peace, liberty, and artistic expression. His entertaining novel *Candide* showed the wildness of a world that is not closely managed by God. For Voltaire, a perfect God made the world, just as a watchmaker makes a watch. Then the world, like the watch, could simply run according to its design. Understanding that design was the theme of the Enlightenment.

No one pursued that theme with more energy than the French philosopher Denis Diderot, who collected a huge body of rationalist writings by contemporary philosophers into his *Encyclopedia*, published between 1751 and 1772. His concept was bold; he intended to summarize all of human knowledge.

Despite the power and appeal of Enlightenment ideas and works, they did not reach the masses of people during that time. The everyday lives of 17th- and 18th-century Europeans were undoubtedly influenced more by traditional Christian beliefs than by the ideas of the Enlightenment philosophers. Nevertheless, a new, popular literature was spreading rapidly during this period, especially in Spain, where Cervantes's novel *Don Quixote* presented universal themes in a distinctly Spanish setting.

2. ENLIGHTENMENT IDEAS IN ARTS AND SCIENCES

Enlightenment writers emphasized human reason and its power to make life better. One of the most influential historical studies ever done, Edward Gibbon's *The History of the Decline and Fall of the Roman Empire*, published in 1776, explained the rise of Christianity in purely rational terms. Other scholars went further in praising virtue and reason while criticizing religion. They taught ethics (ideas about right and wrong) as a matter of balance and harmony, and they drew heavily from the ancient Greek and Roman philosophers. Painters followed this trend in what was called the "neoclassical style." The French painter Jacques-Louis David (dah-VEED, 1748–1825) used Roman stories to depict fundamental virtues such as patriotism.

While major composers continued to write music on religious themes, such as Haydn's *The Creation* and Mozart's *Requiem*, they also created other forms, such as operas with ancient Roman settings and contemporary Enlightenment themes.

SUMMING UP

Beginning around 1500, European monarchs began to gain power. The weakening of the feudal system, the rise of cities, the growth of the middle class and trade, and colonization all supported the monarch in his or her struggle to overcome the power of the nobility and the Church. Some monarchs achieved absolute power: they controlled their kingdom's wealth and laws without visible resistance. Louis XIV, Frederick the Great, and Peter the Great all were successful in gathering power to themselves and creating absolute monarchies. Their supreme kingly power was soon to become the target of a new wave of reforms, in the Enlightenment.

During the 16th, 17th, and 18th centuries, Europe witnessed the birth of modern science. The Scientific Revolution, which began with a challenge to the commonly accepted notion that the earth was the center of the universe, ultimately overthrew many ideas about the world and the universe. The most revolutionary idea put forward by the new science, however, was that the truth about the universe could be discovered by observing and experimenting. Observation and experimentation led to more and more discoveries and advances in all fields of study. Today, they still form the basis of scientific method and of our understanding of the world around us. Scientific study of government led to revolutionary new theories that in turn produced political revolutions in England, the American colonies, and France, and later in Central and South America.

CHAPTER REVIEW

1. Absolute monarchy means that
   a. church authority is dominant over the monarch.
   b. the monarch rules without councils or assistants.
   c. the monarch guarantees absolute protection of citizen rights.
   d. the monarch has total control of laws and finances.

2. Which of the following strengthened the power of kings?

   a. the increasing power of feudal lords

   b. the unchallenged authority of the Catholic Church

   c. growth of the middle class and increase in trade

   d. the rise of parliamentary democracy

3. Louis XIV declared that his power to rule came directly from the

   a. will of God.

   b. Council of Ministers.

   c. will of the people.

   d. blessings of the pope.

4. Peter the Great is most remembered for

   a. replacing the Orthodox Church with the Roman Catholic Church.

   b. bringing Western ideas to Russia.

   c. eliminating the influence of the nobility in political affairs.

   d. being concerned for the interests of all Russians.

5. All of the following were factors in the rise of absolute monarchy *except*

   a. the weakening of the feudal system.

   b. the rise of cities.

   c. the rise of trade and the beginnings of colonization.

   d. increasing authority of the Church leadership.

6. The Glorious Revolution of 1688 was important because it

   a. brought Westernization to Russia.

   b. was a step toward limiting the power of the monarch.

   c. began a movement toward religious freedom.

   d. led directly to the Age of Enlightenment.

7. A major cause of the French Revolution was

   a. the increasing power of the middle class.

   b. the refusal of the king to help the American war for independence.

   c. the special privileges of the aristocracy and the clergy.

   d. the absolute power of the Estates General over government finances.

8. Galileo, Copernicus, and Kepler were all concerned with

   a. astronomy and physics.

   b. anatomy and the circulation of blood.

   c. conducting new experiments with chemical compounds.

   d. experimenting with electricity.

9. All of the following ideas helped fuel 18th-century revolutions *except*

   a. life and liberty are natural rights.

   b. people have the right to rise up against abusive governments.

   c. government powers should be separated among branches of the government.

   d. the working class should have more power.

Chapter 7

Politics of the 19th Century

Virginia Standard of Learning WHII.7

The student will demonstrate knowledge of political and philosophical developments in Europe during the 19th century by

a. **assessing the impact of Napoleon and the Congress of Vienna, including changes in political boundaries after 1815.**

b. **describing the influence of revolutions on the expansion of political rights in Europe.**

c. **explaining events related to the unification of Italy and the role of Italian nationalists.**

d. **explaining events related to the unification of Germany and the role of Bismarck.**

Standard WHII.7 a. Napoleon's legacy and the Congress of Vienna

Setting the Scene

The French Revolution launched more than 25 years of conflict in Europe. Revolutionary France went to war with Britain and its other European neighbors. With the rise of Napoleon Bonaparte, the warfare continued. Napoleon kept many of the reforms of the revolution, to which he added a uniform set of laws. These laws, called the **Napoleonic Code**, still form the basis of the French legal system. From 1807 until 1812, Napoleon ruled continental Europe as far east as Poland, but he was never able to achieve his goal of invading Britain. In 1812, he invaded Russia, where he suffered his most costly defeat, the loss of 400,000 men. He raised another army but lost to Britain and its allies in 1814. Following Napoleon's defeat, European leaders gathered in Vienna, Austria, to decide how Europe would reset its borders without French control.

Meanwhile, Napoleon was exiled to Elba, an island a few miles off Italy. He escaped back to France, however, where he raised another army and fought Britain and its allies again. He finally lost at Waterloo (in Belgium) in 1815. This time Napoleon was exiled for good—on the island of St. Helena in the South Atlantic, hundreds of miles from the nearest land.

Key Questions for Standard WHII.7 a

1. **Why did the Congress of Vienna meet?**
2. **What were the results of the Congress of Vienna?**

1. CALLING THE CONGRESS OF VIENNA

The Congress of Vienna was convened to reorganize Europe after the first defeat of Napoleon in 1814. It included the major European nations (except for France), and its leader was Prince Klemens von Metternich of Austria. Metternich was a powerful diplomat who argued persuasively for a return to the stability and security of Europe before the French Revolution. He held strong **conservative** beliefs, including respect for political authority and organized religion and hatred for revolutions. The diplomats and leaders of government wanted a way to handle disputes without resorting to costly and devastating wars.

The leaders of the Congress were stunned by Napoleon's escape from Elba and return to power in France in February 1815. Now the leaders were more convinced than ever to support Metternich's conservative ideas.

Europe before the Congress of Vienna.

2. RESULTS OF THE CONGRESS OF VIENNA

The Congress of Vienna "turned back the hands of time." Alarmed by the French Revolution's political chaos and military aggression, the leaders of Europe restored monarchies in Austria and Prussia and created the kingdom of the Netherlands. These were conservative steps, designed to suppress democracy, control the French, and put Europe back the way it had been in 1789. The Congress supported monarchies and the traditional class system. To keep Europe in order, the Congress also promoted a **balance of power** among the European nations. Thus, it allowed France to remain a powerful country, just *not the most powerful country*.

After the Congress of Vienna, Europe was without war for more than 35 years. Almost immediately, however, its conservative decisions came into conflict with a growing desire for greater political freedom.

Standard WHII.7 b. Revolutions and political rights in Europe

Setting the Scene

After years of fighting with France, the diplomats at the Congress of Vienna wanted to return to what they saw as the stability and security of Europe before the French Revolution. People all over Europe, however, were enthusiastic about ideas of independence, both for themselves and for their countries.

The monarchs who were returned to power proved not to be very good rulers, a trend that only inflamed the feelings for revolution that the monarchs wanted to suppress. These revolutionary feelings came to be called **liberalism**, and liberals

Europe after the Congress of Vienna.

strongly supported parliamentary government. Britain was unwilling to suppress revolutions on the continent of Europe. On the other hand, Austria, Prussia, Russia, and France were quite willing to use force against revolutionary movements in any European country.

The clash between the forces for change and the forces in power came to a head in 1848. Revolutions broke out mainly in the growing cities, where many thousands of people could easily join together to attack government offices.

Key Questions for Standard WHII.7 b

1. **What were the revolutions of 1848?**
2. **How did urbanization affect the expansion of democracy in 19th-century Europe?**

1. THE REVOLUTIONS OF 1848

As liberalism grew stronger, revolution spread across Europe in 1848. That year, all of the major European nations, except for Britain and Russia, experienced explosions of revolutionary violence. France was the scene of the greatest violence. Fighting also broke out in the major cities of Germany, Italy, and Hungary, and in the dominant power of central Europe, Austria. The revolutions failed to create lasting democratic governments, but Europe's monarchs began to realize that they could not put down people's demands forever. Many ordinary citizens had made it clear that they wanted to play an important part in the way their countries were governed.

A small book with large impact over time, Karl Marx's *Communist Manifesto*, was published in 1848. Its rousing language (including "Workingmen of all countries, unite") and its emphasis on how laborers under capitalism were being exploited made it truly revolutionary. Though it appears to have had little influence on the events of 1848, it was the clearest and most dramatic statement of Marx's revolutionary theories. Communist leaders to the present day credit Marx as the source of their **ideology**.

2. URBANIZATION AND THE EXPANSION OF DEMOCRACY

The 19th century in Europe was a period of steadily increasing population. In the most **industrialized** countries—Britain, France, Germany, and the Netherlands—the growing populations were drawn to the cities to work in the new factories there. This process, called **urbanization**, had several results that were particularly notable in the first country to industrialize, Britain:

- *Decline of rural populations*. Countries that had been mainly rural now had more and more of their people living in large cities.
- *Growing political influence of the urban middle class*. As industry and commerce expanded, more people could get jobs above the lowest laboring level and make enough money to live in relative comfort. Men in the British middle class, which was larger and more influential than in other countries, urged their government to extend the vote so that more of them would be represented in the House of Commons, the lower house of Parliament.
- *More representation for cities*. Britain's electoral districts had been drawn up when the country was still mainly rural. After the Industrial Revolution, a small rural district could still have a representative in the House of Commons while a mushrooming city of tens of thousands had none. A series of reform laws in Britain gave representation to more towns and cities.

Overall, the trend in 19th-century Britain was toward democratic reform. The House of Commons increased its power, and its membership became more representative of the general population of the country (women still could not vote, however.) The British also showed increased concern for human rights by prohibiting the transatlantic slave trade and using their navy to hunt down slave traders.

Standard WHII.7 c. Garibaldi and the unification of Italy

Setting the Scene

In the mid-1800s, Italy was divided into about a half dozen large states and a few small states. Austria controlled northern Italy, while foreign monarchs ruled southern Italy. Italians became increasingly frustrated with living under foreign rule. They also desired a return to the greatness associated with the Roman empire and with the Italian Renaissance. They were swept by a feeling of **nationalism**—of wanting one united nation.

Key Questions for Standard WHII.7 c

1. **Why did Italian states unite around the state of Sardinia?**
2. **How did Garibaldi move Italian unification close to completion?**

1.   ITALIAN STATES UNITE AROUND SARDINIA

From 1852 on, many Italians saw the Kingdom of Sardinia as a good possibility to lead and unify the Italian states. The Prime Minister of Sardinia, Count Camillo di Cavour (kah-VOOR), was a capable leader who strengthened Sardinia's finances and army. In order to throw off Austrian control of other parts of Italy, Cavour needed outside help. In 1859, he got help from the French to push the Austrians out of most of Italy. As a result, some northern Italian states became part of the Kingdom of Sardinia.

2.   GARIBALDI

Cavour's moves showed Italian revolutionaries, notably Giuseppe Garibaldi, the possibilities of the situation. Garibaldi raised an army of 100,000 volunteers, called Red Shirts, and captured most of Sicily. After Garibaldi's forces moved onto the Italian peninsula, they captured Naples and the rest of southern Italy. Due to the efforts of Cavour and Garibaldi, most of Italy was unified by 1861, except for

During 1859–1870, individual states combined to form a unified Italy.

the Papal States, which occupied over a hundred miles of the west coast of Italy.

Cavour persuaded Garibaldi not to attack the Papal States, because the pope was under the protection of French forces. Cavour did not want France intervening deeper into Italy. In 1870, though, the last French troops left the Papal States. Soon, Italy **annexed** Rome, which became that country's capital.

Standard WHII.7 d. Bismarck and the unification of Germany

Setting the Scene

The 19th-century rise of liberalism was accompanied by a dramatic increase in nationalism. To nationalists, the bonds of common language, history, religion, culture, and territory were passionately important. These feelings strengthened the desire for a government that represented the people who shared such bonds.

The German states, all 39 of them, maintained their independence until the mid-1800s. Prussia and Austria were the leading German states, and they competed for domination of the others. In 1871, Prussia won out because of its united population, its industrialization, and its prime minister, Otto von Bismarck.

Key Questions for Standard WHII.7 d

1. **What role did Otto von Bismarck play in the unification of Germany?**
2. **How is Bismarck remembered?**

1. THE UNIFICATION OF GERMANY

Otto von Bismarck became the prime minister of Prussia in 1862, and from that time until 1871 he took bold steps to unify Germany. In 1864, he joined with Austria to take territory from Denmark. In 1866, he provoked a war with Austria, which the Prussians won in six weeks. This victory was so convincing that Prussia became the dominant state of Germany. Most of the German states then joined with Prussia in a North German Confederation.

The French were uneasy about the power of the Confederation. In 1870, Bismarck tricked the French into war (known as the Franco-Prussian War). Just as he had calculated, the southern German states joined the Confederation, and the Germans easily defeated the French, even capturing Paris after a short siege. By these bold moves (especially German victory in the Franco-Prussian War), Bismarck pulled the German states together into the German nation, completing the process in 1871.

2. HISTORICAL EVALUATION OF BISMARCK

Bismarck was one of the two most influential Europeans of the 19th century. (The other was Napoleon.) He is admired for his success in bringing the German states together, but he has been criticized for his deceptions and for his use of force. He has been called great, but also ruthless. He will always be associated with **realpolitik** (the "politics of reality"). This is the belief that politics should be based not on ideals but on whatever works best to benefit the nation. Thus, Bismarck is often cited as an example of the powerful, practical prince described by Machiavelli (discussed in Chapter 2).

SUMMING UP

Revolutionary France was the dominant European power at the beginning of the 19th century. After Napoleon's defeat, the 1815 Congress of

By 1871, individual states had combined to form a unified Germany.

Vienna established a balance of power among Britain, France, Austria, Prussia, and Russia. Then wars and revolutions disrupted the balance, as Italy unified into a nation and Prussia became the great power Germany. Meanwhile, Britain steadily increased its economic and military strength. By the end of the 19th century, Europe had two leading powers, Germany and Britain, and a dangerous rivalry had begun.

CHAPTER REVIEW

1. The purpose of the Congress of Vienna in 1815 was to

   a. create an alliance to defeat the forces of Napoleon.

   b. formulate a plan to recapture Napoleon after his escape from Elba.

   c. restore the European order the way it was prior to 1789.

   d. promote the unification of Italy.

2. The Battle of Waterloo in June 1815 is one of the most significant European events of the 19th century because

   a. Napoleon's defeat led to a new balance of power that prevented war for 35 years.

   b. the battle led directly to European recognition of American independence.

   c. it opened the way for Napoleon's forces to invade Russia and reach all the way to Moscow.

   d. it broke the power of the British-Prussian alliance and altered the balance of power in Europe in favor of France and Austria.

3. All of the following were actions of the Congress of Vienna *except*

   a. restoring monarchies.

   b. promoting a balance of power.

   c. reducing French power.

   d. promoting republican governments.

4. All of the following nations experienced revolutionary uprisings in their cities in the mid-19th century *except*

   a. France.

   b. Germany.

   c. Austria.

   d. Britain.

5. In the *Communist Manifesto*, German author Karl Marx

   a. challenged the authority of the Church-state relationship.

   b. criticized the capitalist exploitation of labor.

   c. warned against the future impact of revolutionary change.

   d. defended the concept of private property and the profit motive.

6. An important result of 19th-century urbanization in Britain was

   a. an increase in agricultural production.

   b. a demand for reform and more equal representation in Parliament.

   c. a shrinking of the middle-class population.

   d. a movement for more parliamentary representation for rural areas.

7. Otto von Bismarck and Giuseppe Garibaldi are remembered as

   a. early Communist revolutionary leaders in Germany and France.

   b. advocates for the vote for non-landowning peasants.

   c. architects of national unification in Germany and Italy.

   d. founders of the earliest workers' rights movements in central Europe.

Chapter

8

The Industrial Revolution

Virginia Standard of Learning WHII.8
The student will demonstrate knowledge of the effects of the Industrial Revolution during the 19th century by

a. **citing scientific, technological, and industrial developments and explaining how they brought about urbanization and social and environmental changes.**

b. **explaining the emergence of capitalism as a dominant economic pattern, and the subsequent development of socialism and communism.**

c. **describing the evolution of the nature of work and the labor force, including its effects on families, the status of women and children, the slave trade, and the labor union movement.**

d. **explaining the rise of industrial economies and their link to imperialism and nationalism.**

e. **assessing the impact of European economic and military power on Asia and Africa, with emphasis on the competition for resources and the responses of colonized peoples.**

Standard WHII.8 a. How science, technology, and industry changed Europe

Setting the Scene

The British and the French both established successful industries before the French Revolution. The textile industry was especially successful, as was the mining and production of metals. Great Britain was the home of the most important inventions, with the exception of the Frenchman Joseph Jacquard's (zhah-KAR) silk loom. (This an- ticipated a 20th-century invention by using punched cards to control the machine. Early computers used punched cards through the 1960s.)

The **Industrial Revolution** greatly expanded production. The industrialized countries therefore looked for more sources of raw materials and more markets in which to sell their manufactured goods. They found both by taking over distant lands as colonies. Meanwhile, at home in the industrialized countries, populations increased, transportation improved, cities grew, and the middle class became larger and better educated.

Key Questions for Standard WHII.8 a

1. **Why did some nations develop extensive industries in the 19th century?**

2. **How did new inventions drive the Industrial Revolution?**

1. THE DEVELOPMENT OF INDUSTRY

Industrialization has two main components: **power-driven machinery** and the **factory system**. In the 19th century, these replaced handicrafts as the major production method, first in Britain and Belgium, then in Germany. Russia also developed significant industry by the end of the 19th century but remained primarily an agricultural nation. Industrialization in Germany was helped greatly by heavy railroad construction in the 1850s and 1860s, by the lowering of **trade barriers** among the German states, and then by the uniting of the states into one nation by 1871. France was hindered by its limited deposits of coal and iron.

In addition to its other advantages, Great Britain had stronger financial resources to purchase machinery and build factories than any other European nation. While in Britain government regulation caused few problems for manufacturers, in France government regulation was extensive and restrictive. A well-developed system of British canals further supported that nation's industries, since water transportation was, at first, the most efficient way to get industrial products to market. Later, railroads moved both people and products. In 1804, the British began transporting coal by steam-powered train and 21 years later opened the first railroad to carry passengers. Finally, the Enclosure Movement in Britain took away from many farmers the traditional right to use fields and common pastures on manor farms.

Thus, many farmers, lacking land, had to take jobs in factories or mines, providing a new pool of labor for the expanding industries.

2. NEW INVENTIONS

Two industries dominated the early phase of the Industrial Revolution. The first was mining and the production of metals. Iron was necessary to build the new machines, and iron ore was needed to produce it. One breakthrough was Abraham Darby's discovery of a method for producing the extreme heat needed for smelting iron by using coke, a product made from coal. A second breakthrough was Thomas Newcomen's development of a steam engine that could pump water out of the mines. These 18th-century inventions were dramatically enhanced in 1856 when Henry Bessemer invented the steel "converter" to remove impurities for making cheaper, better steel. Steel now replaced iron (which was cheaper but weaker and heavier) in many machines and structures.

The second of the two key industries was textiles. Improvements in the textile industry came like a chain reaction. It all began in 1733 when John Kay built a machine to weave cloth. His "flying shuttle" replaced the slow process of pushing the shuttle by hand. Then one improvement led to another (see the table). James Watt improved Newcomen's steam engine so that it could be used to drive factory machines. James Hargreaves and Samuel Crompton mechanized the spinning of cotton thread.

Though these two industries were at the center of the Industrial Revolution, many other areas of production were improved and speeded up in similar ways. The **factory system** was itself an invention that replaced hand labor in homes. The factory system put work-

18th-Century Textile Inventors and Their Inventions

1733	John Kay	flying shuttle	speeded up weaving
1768	Richard Arkwright	water frame	water power for spinning
1765	James Watt	improved steam engine	steam power for textile machines
1770	James Hargreaves	spinning Jenny	speeded up spinning
1779	Samuel Crompton	spinning mule	combined steam engine, Jenny, and water frame

ers and machines together under one roof with a steady supply of **raw materials**, a disciplined work schedule, and an efficient means of distributing the goods. An American named Eli Whitney improved the system by designing **interchangeable parts** for factory production of guns, removing much of the custom work and speeding up production. As the factory system was applied to a variety of industries, demand for raw materials increased.

Standard WHII.8 b, c. Early capitalism and the responses of socialism and communism

Setting the Scene

The new productivity of industries was organized according to the economic system of capitalism. Capitalism relies upon the open competition among manufacturers and merchants to set prices and working conditions. In this early capitalism, the well-being of the workers was of little concern. Hours in a workweek were long, and working conditions were poor. Still, capitalism was associated with freedom as well as profits. Adam Smith argued in *The Wealth of Nations* (1776) that the best way to create economic growth was to give individuals the freedom to pursue their economic needs. Smith's defense of capitalism was hugely persuasive and remained influential in the 19th

and 20th centuries, even as the problems of unregulated capitalism became more evident.

Key Questions for Standard WHII.8 b, c

1. **What effects did the Industrial Revolution have on people in Europe?**
2. **What movements developed in response to industrialism and capitalism?**

1. EFFECTS OF THE INDUSTRIAL REVOLUTION

The Industrial Revolution was a powerful pressure for urbanization. Many people moved to the cities to work in factories. In cities, they were forced to purchase food, clothing, and other supplies, since they usually had no time or opportunity to produce these for themselves. They depended entirely on the value of their labor to the factory owners, and the factory owners could set low wages since there were nearly always more job seekers than jobs. Owners of mines and factories had control over the lives of their laborers. Thus, the Industrial Revolution brought new wealth and comfort to some people but social disruption and exploitation to many more. Government leaders shared the views of Adam Smith, who in his *The Wealth of Nations* argued that the state should stay out of economic matters.

As a result, capitalism generally developed in this **laissez-faire** (hands-off) manner, and extreme wealth developed beside grim poverty.

Governments' "hands-off" approaches to the operation of new factories also led to the problem of environmental pollution. Factory furnaces blew waste products into the air, and pumped waste chemicals into nearby rivers and canals. For example, a royal investigation in Britain in 1866 found that the water in the town of Calder could be used as ink with which to write. Moreover, it was reported, the nearby Bradford Canal was so full of chemicals that it could be set on fire with a match. These were extreme cases, but they represented problems that have continued in some parts of the world into the 21st century.

The upheavals of the Industrial Revolution also brought benefits that gradually spread to more and more people. Factories produced goods more cheaply than they could be made by hand. Faster and cheaper transportation helped distribute these goods to more people. Since these developments also made slavery economically obsolete, Britain and the United States outlawed first the slave trade and then slavery.

As more people were freed from the dusk-to-dawn rural work schedule, some of them began to receive an education. Freeing up time in young people's lives made it possible to extend schooling beyond the very wealthy families. Private schools met this need in the early

Women and children were employed in large numbers in British factories in the 19th century.

19th century, but public schools were widespread in Germany, France, Britain, and the United States by the end of the 19th century.

By this time, too, many people were living healthier lives. Most of the important improvements in public health up to the middle of the 19th century resulted from better housing, sanitation facilities, and nutrition. A few medical breakthroughs, though, had dramatic effects. Edward Jenner's systematic use of a smallpox vaccine began the long process of eliminating smallpox as a natural hazard. Meanwhile, Louis Pasteur's work in identifying bacteria and describing their characteristics started doctors down a path of understanding infections, using antiseptic techniques, and eventually discovering antibiotics.

Changing roles of women and children. Despite the new opportunities noted above, the role that women and children played in 19th-century industry was a difficult one. The textile industry employed many women and children because they could be paid less than men and because their small hands were useful for performing tasks around moving machine parts. Children were also exploited as miners, where small size had advantages in cramped underground tunnels.

While hard work was not new to women or children in the 19th century, industrialization brought them out of their homes and into factories and mines, undermining their well-being and disrupting family life. By 1900, factories in Britain and the United States were filled with orphaned and impoverished children.

2. RESPONSES TO THE INDUSTRIAL REVOLUTION AND CAPITALISM

Labor unions. One major counterbalance to the power of industrial capitalism was the rise of **labor unions**. These unions organized workers to resist unfair treatment. They strengthened the workers in dealings with the owners by enabling them to bargain collectively rather than individually for their needs. By striking—refusing to work—the unionized workers could pressure the owners to increase wages and improve working conditions. The unions also lobbied their governments for laws to improve workers' lives.

Unions faced strong opposition, since many people felt that they were contrary to the laws of capitalism and disrupted the natural order of society. Owners did not want to share control of their factories with their workers.

The antislavery movement. Textile factories in Great Britain were supplied with raw cotton from the Southern United States. As new machines made textile production more profitable, cotton growing expanded—and so did the demand for slaves to pick it. The South became more dependent on slaves and built a defense of slavery into its social philosophy. The American antislavery movement was therefore a challenge to the textile industry, and the outbreak of the American Civil War created a dilemma for the British, who had already banned slavery in their colonies, in 1833. In the end, Great Britain did not support the South in the U.S. Civil War, and it relied on India for raw cotton for its factories.

Socialist responses to the Industrial Revolution. Socialists criticized the new industrial capitalism. Under **socialism**, the system they favored, there is public (government) ownership of the major industries. **Communism** originally meant the same thing, but it has come to be associated also with government control of people's lives and the use of violence as a means to accomplish its goals.

Two forms of socialism arose in the first half of the 19th century. One was **utopian** (from Sir Thomas More's *Utopia*, a 16th-century book about an "ideal" society), and the other was **Marxian**. Utopian socialists extended the basic idea of the Enlightenment—to make society more equal and productive over time through the use of reason. Marxian socialists advocated sudden change as a result of worker uprisings.

- *Utopian socialists.* The most famous utopian was Robert Owen. He attempted to show that factories could be run profitably even when their workers received better working conditions, higher pay, and better housing than was typical in the early 19th century. Owen had some success with his methods at his cotton mill in New Lanark, Scotland. He had less success with his U.S. project at New Harmony, Indiana.

- *Marxian socialists.* Karl Marx wrote that the pursuit of economic goals drove history and that the most important events were signs of struggle between economic classes. Marxian socialists believed that no real progress could be made until wealth was redistributed from the factory owners to their workers. Marx's *Communist Manifesto* (1848) called for a worker uprising, while his much longer *Das Kapital* (1867) laid out an economic theory that was later adopted by revolutionaries in Russia, and then still later by revolutionaries in China, Cuba, and other places around the world. Thus, Marxian socialism, or communism as it came to be called, became a powerful political force. It continues to be influential in China, Cuba, North Korea, Laos, and Vietnam.

Standard WHII.8 d, e. The effects of European power on Asia and Africa

Setting the Scene

With the rise of industry in Europe and elsewhere in the 19th century, products could be manufac-

tured in far greater quantities than ever before. Thus, there was an increasing need for natural resources. These included coal and water to drive steam-powered machinery and raw materials (such as metal ores) from which to manufacture the products. With their increasing output, European and American manufacturers also wanted wider markets for their goods. As a result, industrial nations looked around the world for sources of raw materials and new markets.

Europeans and Americans often attempted to justify their involvement in Asia and Africa in altruistic (unselfish) terms. Though many Christian missionaries worked in Africa and Asia, the primary motive of the 19th-century European powers was economic gain.

Key Questions for Standard WHII.8 d, e

1. **Why and how did Europeans colonize Asia and Africa?**
2. **How did people in Asia and Africa respond to colonization?**

1. COLONIZING ASIA AND AFRICA

European nations competed with one another for control of markets and sources of raw materials. Two important targets were Asia and Africa.

Asia. European **imperialism** in Asia began in the 17th and the 18th centuries and then expanded dramatically in the 19th century. The French and British expanded their power in India in the 18th century. However, the British became the dominant force there after defeating France in the Seven Years' War in 1763. The British East India Company then took control of parts of India.

The British imported tea and cotton from India, and forbade the development of Indian industry. India was Britain's "Jewel in the

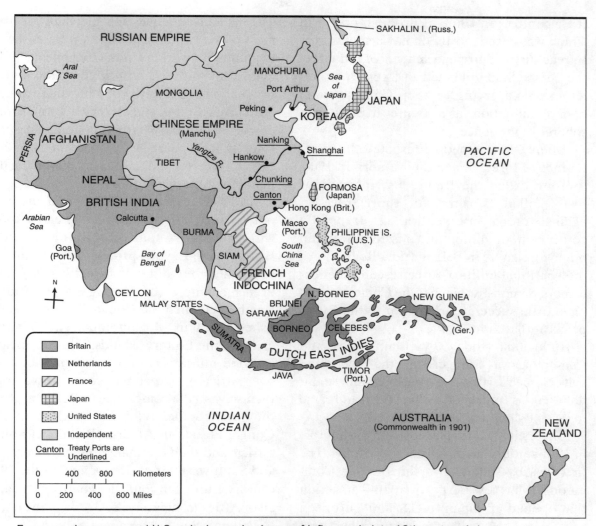

European, Japanese, and U.S. colonies and spheres of influence in late 19th-century Asia.

Crown," but the British disrupted Indian culture and were deeply resented. In the mid-1880s, a group of Indians took an important step toward their future independence by founding the Indian National Congress party, led by Mohandas Gandhi. Though the British later made important technical improvements in India, especially by the building of railroads, a current of anti-British feeling remained strong right up to independence in 1947.

In China, the British discovered that they could trade the addictive drug opium for Chinese goods. When Chinese officials burned chests of opium in British warehouses in Guangzhou in 1839, the act set off what was known as the Opium War. The British defeated the Chinese easily, forcing the opening of Chinese ports to British trade. Then Britain defeated the Chinese again in the Second Opium War, in 1856. Over time Britain, the Netherlands, Russia, France, and Germany all established **spheres of influence** (areas under their control) in China. European power in China was based mostly on naval superiority. In reaction to European spheres of influence, the United States pursued an Open Door policy in China, trying to keep Chinese trade open to all nations as a counter to European spheres of influence.

Many Chinese people resented the interference of foreigners in their affairs. In 1900, a group called the Righteous Harmonious Fists (called "Boxers" for short) rose up against foreign intervention and trapped a contingent of diplomats, missionaries, and other foreigners in Peking (now Beijing). An international military force rescued the foreigners, demonstrating that the Chinese would have little success standing up to the Europeans at that time.

Indochina (today's Vietnam, Laos, and Cambodia) was conquered by the French, despite fierce resistance by the Vietnamese. Indonesia was controlled by the Dutch and came to be called the Dutch East Indies.

The United States played an important role in 19th-century imperialism in two ways. The first was by sending warships under Commodore Matthew Perry to Japan—an action that opened up Japan to U.S. and European trade. Since the 1640s, the Japanese had kept foreign merchants out of the country in an effort to protect traditional Japanese customs. In 1853, Perry reopened trade with Japan, prompting the Japanese to develop Western-style military and industrial power.

The second important U.S. action was the defeat of Spain in 1898 in the Spanish-American War. As a result of this war, the United States took control of Cuba, Puerto Rico, and the Philippines.

Africa. The Atlantic slave trade was Europe's first (but not last) commercial pursuit with disastrous consequences for Africans. At first, most of the captured Africans were enslaved as plantation workers in the Caribbean. However, Eli Whitney's cotton gin made cotton production extremely profitable in the Southern United States, and slavery became firmly entrenched in the South's economy and philosophy. In Britain, slave traders financed and expanded cotton mills, which increased the demand for American raw cotton.

In 1830, France invaded Algeria and held onto it after a fierce struggle. Then by 1869, with the Suez Canal recently opened, the British made Egypt a **protectorate** (an area it controlled but did not directly rule). The French countered by pushing into the Sudan. Belgium claimed the Congo. Portugal established itself in Mozambique. The Spanish claimed the Canary Islands. The Europeans avoided military conflict with one another over Africa by agreeing to carve it up among themselves. At a conference in Berlin in 1884, they staked their claims—Belgium in the Congo, France in Algeria, Britain in South Africa, and then Germany in the Cameroons and Southwest Africa. By the end of the 19th century, European countries controlled nearly all of Africa from France's Algeria in the north to Britain's South Africa in the south.

2. ASIAN AND AFRICAN RESPONSES

In the 19th century, European imperialism provoked anticolonial movements and, in some cases, armed rebellions such as the Sepoy Mutiny of 1857. Sepoys were Indian soldiers in the British army. These men held deep grievances against their British officers. Their rebellion spread throughout northern and central India, and it took the British more than a year to subdue the Sepoys. The violence led to reforms in the way the British ruled India.

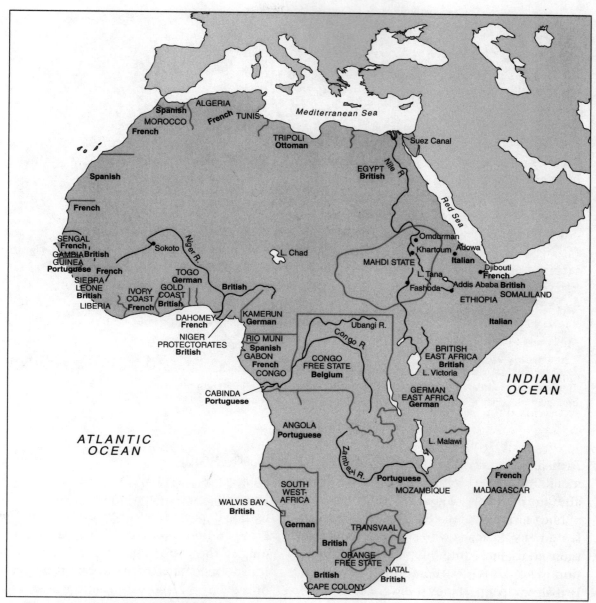

European colonies in 19th-century Africa.

As a rule, the modern weapons used by Europeans made African and Asian resistance to imperialism costly and ineffective. Only Ethiopia fought back successfully against the Europeans, defeating an Italian invasion in 1896. More typical was the Battle of Omdur-man in the Sudan in 1898. There, 40,000 Sudanese attacked a British and Egyptian force. In the battle, 11,000 Sudanese were killed, while the British lost 48 men.

In Southern Africa, Dutch settlers called Afrikaners were joined by large numbers of

The uprising of Indian soldiers in 1857 against their British commanders shocked Great Britain into changing its policy toward India. Here Indian prisoners are being punished by the British.

British, especially after the discovery of diamonds at Kimberley in 1868 and even more so after the discovery of gold in the Afrikaner republic of Transvaal in 1886. British forces defeated any Africans who stood in the way of their goals, including the powerful Zulu nation. The Dutch settlers rebelled against British control, and they too were defeated by the British, in a conflict called the Boer War (1899–1902).

The intellectual response of colonized peoples to imperialism proved to be the most important. After suffering under European nationalistic ambitions, Asians and Africans developed strong nationalistic movements of their own, and these have resulted in numerous independent, modern countries.

SUMMING UP

During this period, Western European and U.S. factories powered up with water and steam and used that power to run a collection of machines grouped under one roof. This was the beginning of the factory system. Industrialization transformed much of the world quickly, and all of it over time. Industrialization gave the Europeans and Americans influence overseas on a scale never before possible. Powerful navies brought troops and traders to Asia and Africa, where they disrupted traditional societies as they planted seeds of modernization. Industrialization transformed the powerful nations too, moving them from rural to urban societies and creating new wealthy and middle classes alongside a new urban poor. For many people, the standard of living rose. For many others, the vision of Western wealth and power became both a hated symbol and a desired goal. The stage was set for explosive conflict and change in the 20th century.

CHAPTER REVIEW

1. The first successful industry to use machinery for processing raw materials and manufacturing finished products was the
   a. metal industry for smelting iron into steel.
   b. textile industry for converting wool and cotton fiber into cloth.
   c. armaments industry for mass-producing muskets and rifles.
   d. mining industry for revolutionizing the production of coal and iron ore.

2. Which nation had the greatest advantages for industrial growth?
   a. France
   b. Netherlands
   c. Germany
   d. Great Britain

3. The new source of power that revolutionized 19th-century industry was
   a. gasoline power.
   b. water power.
   c. wind power.
   d. steam power.

4. What valuable resources from India helped make the British empire the wealthiest in the world?
   a. tin and copper
   b. tea and cotton
   c. rubber
   d. petroleum

5. The United States played an important role in 19th-century imperialism by
   a. ending the opium trade with China.
   b. opening Japan to Western trade and influence.
   c. crushing the Sepoy Mutiny in India.
   d. establishing control of the East Indies trade route.

6. The slave trade from Africa to North America was stimulated by
   a. the growth of the cotton and textile industries.
   b. the innovation of steam-driven ships.
   c. the opening of the Suez Canal.
   d. the labor demands of tea and spice plantations.

7. Nineteenth-century critics of the Industrial Revolution were particularly concerned about
   a. the expense of new machinery.
   b. the influx of immigrant labor.
   c. the high cost of manufactured goods.
   d. the exploitation of women and children.

8. The most significant world change from an agricultural economy to an industrial economy occurred between what years?
   a. 1500 and 1600
   b. 1600 and 1700
   c. 1700 and 1800
   d. 1800 and 1900

ERA **VII**

**Era of Global Wars,
1914 to 1945**

Chapter 9

World War I

Virginia Standard of Learning WHII.9

The student will demonstrate knowledge of the worldwide impact of World War I by

a. **explaining economic and political causes and major events, and by identifying major leaders of the war, with emphasis on Woodrow Wilson and Kaiser Wilhelm II.**

b. **explaining the outcomes and global effects of the war and the Treaty of Versailles.**

c. **citing causes and consequences of the Russian revolutions.**

Standard WHII.9 a–c. Causes, events, and results of World War I

Setting the Scene

Some historians say that the 20th century really began at the start of World War I in 1914, because the war marked the end of one way of life and the beginning of another. Certainly the war changed the way Europeans thought about themselves and about their future. The decade before the war was one of peace and economic growth, and European powers dominated international affairs everywhere except in the Americas. Trade was expanding, and new inventions, such as the automobile, airplane, radio, and movies, were causing excitement. Progress was unstoppable, or so it seemed. For Europeans, this period of high hopes ended with the deadliest war fought up to that time.

Key Questions for Standard WHII.9 a–c

1. **What caused World War I?**

2. **What events influenced the course of the war?**

3. **What were the results of the war?**

4. **What were the results of the Russian revolutions?**

1. CAUSES OF THE WAR

Three main factors pushed the European powers toward war in 1914.

- *Nationalism.* The nationalistic rivalry between France and Germany was especially intense as a result of Bismarck's wars to unify Germany (discussed in Chapter 7). The Germans had defeated France in 1870 and forced France to cede territory to them.
- *The alliance system.* The powers of Europe were divided into two rival camps (discussed below).
- *A combination of **militarism** and imperialism.* Britain, France, Germany, Austria, Italy, and Russia had all expanded their military forces, and all of them had plans for territorial expansion. The German desire for colonies was especially dangerous. Despite having colonies in Africa and spheres of influence in China, the Germans felt that they were behind Britain and France in empire building and were determined to catch up. Competition over colonies increased tensions among the European powers.

Though many of the European rulers contributed to these dangerous conditions, no one played a larger role than the German emperor, Kaiser Wilhelm II (KY-zur VIL-helm). In 1890, Wilhelm dismissed Bismarck, the longtime German Chancellor and master of *realpolitik* (discussed on page 80). Wilhelm took charge of German foreign policy, and he reversed some of Bismarck's most important steps. One major reversal came when Wilhelm ended Germany's alliance with Russia, which then signed an alliance with the French. Wilhelm also reversed Bismarck's policy of not threatening British naval superiority. He began a massive buildup of the German navy, which the British then matched with a buildup of their own. Thus, Wilhelm contributed to Germany's rivalries with both Russia and Britain, adding these to Germany's rivalry with France.

The immediate cause of World War I was the assassination in 1914 of Archduke Franz Ferdinand, heir to the Austrian throne, in the Bosnian city of Sarajevo (sah-rah-YEH-voh). Austria at that time was a large country with a diverse population. The three largest groups were the Germans, the Hungarians, and the Slavs, many of whom lived in the region of Bosnia. The people of neighboring Serbia were Slavs, and they hoped to become leaders of a larger Slavic nation that would include the Bosnians. Many Serbians hated Franz Ferdinand because he wanted to give the Slavs a stronger position within Austria, thus ruining Serbia's plans to lead them.

Serbia had little military power, so any efforts to thwart the Archduke, some Serbians felt, had to involve terrorist violence. A group of men who took this view planned to kill Archduke Franz Ferdinand and his wife Sophie as they toured the city of Sarajevo. One of the assassins, Gavrilo Princip (PREEN-tseep), got an easy shot at the royal couple when their driver entered the wrong street and stopped the car to turn around. The car stopped within five feet of Princip, who fired twice, mortally wounding both the Archduke and his wife.

What followed then was an **ultimatum** (a do-this-or-else demand) from Austria to Serbia demanding, among other things, that the Serbians allow Austrian officials to take part in the criminal proceedings against Princip and the other assassins. At this point, the system of alliances played a part. One alliance, the Triple Alliance, linked Germany, Austria, and Italy. Another, the Triple Entente, linked France, Britain, and Russia.

Before the Austrians pressured the Serbians, they received confirmation that their ally Germany would support whatever demands they made. Russia was pledged to support Serbia, and the Serbian government agreed to only some of the demands. When the Russians **mobilized** their forces (made them ready for war) in support of Serbia, the Germans felt the need to strike first. They activated the Von Schlieffen Plan, by which they hoped to smash through tiny Belgium and defeat France quickly, then turn east to face the Russians. Thus, Europe plunged into war.

One might say that Princip's bullets started the war, but the miscalculations of the European leaders contributed to it. Diplomats of the European powers failed to take the right steps to prevent war. Germany thought that its strong support of Austria would force the Serbians to accept the Austrian ultimatum. The Russians overestimated their own military strength and misjudged the effects of their mobilization. The British failed to convince Germany that British troops would defend Belgium. Still, the worst miscalculation was the view on both sides that whenever war came, it would end quickly and gloriously.

2. IMPORTANT EVENTS OF THE WAR

The war that began in 1914 was long and horrible. It lasted over four years. The Von Schlieffen Plan for German victory failed, partly as a result of heroic resistance by the Belgians,

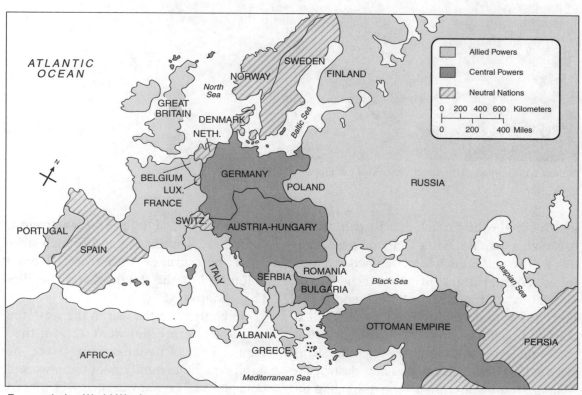

Europe during World War I.

British and German planes in a World War I dogfight.

which bought the French and British time to organize a defense. After Belgium eventually fell, British and French forces launched a well-timed counterattack at the Marne River, which pushed the Germans back and ended their hopes of defeating France quickly. The conflict bogged down into a **war of attrition**, each side trying to wear down the other. Both sides in the conflict developed new destructive weapons: tanks, aircraft, poison gas. When the Russians attacked eastern Germany, the Ger-

mans were forced to fight on two fronts at the same time. The British and French strengthened their armies with troops from their colonies, but the deadlock on the Western Front continued.

In contrast to the war in the west, the war on the Eastern Front went well for the Germans. Since Russian troops were poorly equipped, huge numbers of them were killed or captured. The war was such a disaster for the Russians that it triggered mutinies and contributed to the Russian revolutions of 1917 (discussed on page 103). As a result of the last revolution, Russia quit the war. This enabled Germany to move troops to the Western Front.

In 1917, however, Germany lost more than it gained, because that year the United States entered the war on the side of the British and French. After the Germans resorted to unrestricted submarine warfare in an effort to starve the British, President Woodrow Wilson brought the United States into the war over the issue of freedom of the seas. American troops and equipment proved decisive, and Germany agreed in 1918 to an **armistice** (an end to the fighting). The war killed almost a million British soldiers, between 1 and 2 million French soldiers, between 1 and 2 million German soldiers, and over 5 million Russian soldiers. American losses were far lower.

3. RESULTS OF THE WAR

After the war ended, the victorious powers lost the opportunity for lasting peace. A peace

Britain's Prime Minister David Lloyd George, Italy's Prime Minister Vitorio Orlando, French Premier Georges Clemenceau, and U.S. President Woodrow Wilson (left to right) at the Paris Peace Conference in 1919.

treaty can be an instrument of peace or an instrument of revenge. In the Treaty of Versailles, the leaders of France and Britain chose revenge against Germany. The leaders of smaller nations were excluded from the peace arrangements, while the Big Three created the treaty. The Big Three were:

- Georges Clemenceau (ZHORZH kluh-mahn-SOH), Premier (government leader) of France.
- David Lloyd George, Prime Minister (government leader) of Great Britain.
- Woodrow Wilson, President of the United States.

Wilson had announced Fourteen Points as a platform for the peace. The Fourteen Points were, on the whole, rational and fair. They were, however, in conflict with expectations of the British and French that Germany would be blamed for the war and would pay **reparations** (money to make up for the destruction they had caused). As it turned out, the Germans had no chance to negotiate and had harsh terms imposed on them.

Wilson finally had to put his hopes for a lasting peace on his Fourteenth Point: the establishment of a League of Nations. This international body, Wilson argued, could be the place where problems were worked out and war avoided. The League was approved as part of the Versailles Treaty, but the treaty was never **ratified** (officially confirmed) by the U.S. Senate. Without the United States, and with little power to enforce decisions, the League failed as a serious instrument of peace.

In addition to the Versailles Treaty with Germany, separate treaties were signed with the other defeated nations: Austria, Hungary, Bulgaria, and Turkey. These treaties redrew the map of Europe, but not in ways that would ease ethnic tensions. In his Fourteen Points, Wilson had called for **self-determination**, which would enable (as far as possible) each major ethnic group to have its own nation. Instead, much land was simply taken from defeated nations and given to some of the victors. As a result, border disputes between Germany and Poland, Poland and Lithuania, Poland and Czechoslovakia, Austria and Hungary, and Italy and Yugoslavia caused continuing problems. Ethnic violence during the war also left a bitter legacy, especially the 1915 deportations and massacres of Armenians by Turks.

By the war's end, three empires—the Ottoman, the Austro-Hungarian, and the Russian—had been dismantled, and colonial opposition to European control had increased, especially in the Middle East. In a step that later caused discontent, Britain and France gained Arab support against the Turks by promising independence for national groups within the Ottoman empire. After the war, the two powers dashed those Arab nationalist hopes. France took on Lebanon and Syria while Britain took on Iraq and Palestine as **mandates**, possessions ruled on behalf of the League of Nations.

The war was a troubling experience for many soldiers from the French and British colonies who fought in the trenches of Europe. (Morale in two Indian infantry divisions serving on the Western Front dropped so low that these divisions were withdrawn in 1915.) Most importantly, Europeans and colonials disagreed on the meaning of the colonial war effort. Nationalist leaders in the colonies argued that by fighting to win the war for Britain and France, the colonies had earned their independence. European leaders, by contrast, felt that the war had proved the importance of holding onto their colonies.

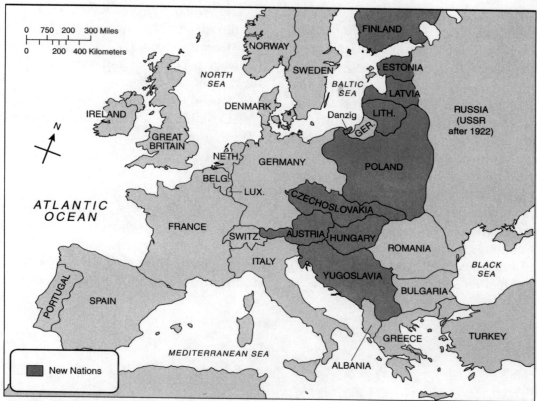

Europe after the war, 1919.

4. THE RUSSIAN REVOLUTIONS

At the start of the 20th century, many Russian people wanted government reforms since they had little confidence in their government. Their confidence was reduced still further by the Russo-Japanese War of 1904, in which the Japanese destroyed the Russian fleet. In 1905, Tsar Nicholas II ruthlessly suppressed a revolution. Though he continued in power, he lost whatever affection the people had for him.

During World War I, conditions in Russia worsened steadily since the Tsar's inefficient government could not handle the two challenges of fighting the Germans and maintaining order at home. Two revolutions occurred in Russia in 1917. The first one, in March,

ended the reign of Tsar Nicholas II; the second, in November, put the Bolshevik (Communist) party in power.

In the first one, frustration with the lack of land for the peasants and with the Tsar's extravagant court life and incompetent war leadership led to the Tsar's overthrow. The Provisional Government, made up of representatives of several political parties, replaced Nicholas. When the Provisional Government made it clear that it would continue the disastrous war against Germany, riots broke out in the capital, St. Petersburg, and the soldiers refused to put them down.

At this point, Vladimir Lenin, exiled leader of the Bolshevik party, returned to Russia. The

Bolsheviks eventually seized power and made peace with the Germans, a move that pleased the war-weary Russian people. Soviet Russia was established with Lenin as its leader. In addition to ending the war with Germany, the Bolsheviks used their new power in Russia to make sweeping changes. They gave control of the factories to the workers, put the banks under state control, and confiscated the property of the Orthodox Church. These measures did not lead to prosperity. In fact, by 1921, Lenin had to face the fact that millions of Russians were starving. In response, he announced a New Economic Policy (N.E.P.) that restored some features of capitalism in an effort to increase production and promote trade.

Meanwhile, the Bolsheviks were engaged in a bloody civil war against White Russians (anti-Communists). By 1922, the Bolsheviks had won this conflict and in that year set up the Union of Soviet Socialist Republics (USSR, also known as the Soviet Union). The USSR combined various nationalities in one large country.

SUMMING UP

Nationalism, militarism, and imperialism, plus a system of alliances that divided Europe into two armed camps, caused World War I. The assassination of Austria-Hungary's Archduke Franz Ferdinand sparked the conflict, which

Addressing Russian troops in Moscow in 1919, V.I. Lenin urged support for the Communist government in the Russian Civil War.

destroyed a generation of Europeans and others in a deadlocked nightmare of artillery, machine-gun, and rifle fire and poison gas and disease. This waste of lives dissolved many people's support for the war, especially in Russia, where first the monarchy, and then the Provisional Government, were overthrown. Communism came to Russia, and Russia left the war in 1917.

Unfortunately for the Germans, the United States entered the war that same year, and U.S. soldiers and materials broke the deadlock. Finally victorious, the French and British sought revenge, while U.S. President Woodrow Wilson tried to build a framework for peace through the League of Nations. The League, however, proved ineffective, partly due to the failure of the United States to join it.

CHAPTER REVIEW

1. All of the following factors helped cause World War I except
   a. nationalist rivalries between France and Germany.
   b. the development of the Triple Alliance and the Triple Entente.
   c. the competition between nations for colonial empires.
   d. the contest between democratic and Communist nations.

2. According to the map on page 99, which of the following nations remained neutral during World War I?
   a. France
   b. Russia
   c. Spain
   d. Germany

3. Archduke Franz Ferdinand was killed by
   a. German nationalists.
   b. Serbian terrorists.
   c. Russian spies.
   d. Austrian rivals.

4. Germany's Von Schlieffen Plan was designed to overcome the problem of
   a. fighting on a strict timetable.
   b. fighting the French and the Russians at the same time.
   c. defeating the superior British navy.
   d. balancing the industrial power of the United States.

5. In 1918, President Wilson proposed a plan for peace that called for the
   a. establishment of alliances to protect Western Europe.
   b. restoration of the monarchies that had been overthrown.
   c. collection of huge war damages from Germany.
   d. settlement of international disputes by a League of Nations.

6. Which of these nations failed to join the League of Nations?
   a. Germany
   b. Britain
   c. United States
   d. France

7. The decision that undermined the Provisional Government in Russia after the first 1917 Revolution was
   a. establishing a secret police organization.
   b. putting workers in control of the factories.
   c. redistributing land.
   d. continuing the war against Germany.

Chapter 10

Between the World Wars

Virginia Standard of Learning WHII.10

The student will demonstrate knowledge of political, economic, social, and cultural developments during the Interwar Period by

a. describing the League of Nations and the mandate system.

b. citing causes and assessing the impact of worldwide depression in the 1930s.

c. examining events related to the rise, aggression, and human costs of totalitarian regimes in the Soviet Union, Germany, Italy, and Japan, and identifying their major leaders, i.e., Joseph Stalin, Adolf Hitler, Benito Mussolini, and Hideki Tojo.

Standard WHII.10 a–c. The League of Nations, worldwide depression, and the rise of dictators

Setting the Scene

As you saw in Chapter 9, the Treaty of Versailles was a treaty of revenge, which was understandable considering the overwhelming suffering caused by World War I. Through the treaty, the victorious nations blamed Germany for the war and sought to make the Germans pay for it. The economics of this were absurd, since the German economy was in collapse. The psychological impact of the treaty was ominous, however, as it fueled German resentments and ambitions. Meanwhile the German economy suffered devastating **inflation** (a general increase in prices) in the 1920s.

Hopes for peace rested on the treaty's provision for a League of Nations. The League had a double responsibility. It had to provide both a way for nations to resolve their differences and a system for ruling some of the territories taken in the war. The difficulties facing the League became enormous with the rise of strong governments willing to use force to increase their power.

Key Questions for Standard WHII.10 a–c

1. **What were the effects of the League of Nations and the mandate system?**

2. **What caused the worldwide economic depression of the 1930s?**

3. **How did totalitarian regimes develop in the Soviet Union, Germany, Italy, and Japan?**

1. THE LEAGUE AND THE MANDATE SYSTEM

President Wilson's Fourteenth Point was the creation of a League of Nations, an international cooperative organization designed to prevent future wars. The other diplomats at Versailles viewed the idea with little enthusiasm, but Wilson refused to give up. The League became a part of each of the treaties ending World War I. The idea behind the League was to preserve peace through international discussions and agreements. The League also controlled the former German colonies and the old Ottoman empire under what was called the "mandate system."

Though the mandate system was supposedly set up to help these areas become independent nations, it became clear that the Europeans wanted to continue their imperialism in Asia and Africa. The British and French believed that their colonies had helped them win the war, and they did not want to give up anything of value.

World War I had spread the idea of self-determination more strongly in Asia than in Africa. The place where European imperialist goals and the colonial peoples' hopes for self-determination clashed most strongly was an area extending from Egypt across the Tigris-Euphrates Valley. There, Europeans tried to replace the defeated Turks as rulers. The Arabic and other Muslim people who lived in this region were embittered by British and French determination to continue their control over the former Ottoman lands and by British support for a Jewish homeland in Palestine.

As an instrument of peace, the League of Nations had a fatal weakness. It had no power to stand up to aggressor nations. It had only "moral force," and against the rising militaristic powers of Italy, Germany, and Japan, this proved to be no force at all. The League was further weakened by the absence of some of the major powers. The Soviet Union was not asked to join at first, and the United States chose not to join at all despite Wilson's role in creating it. The absence of the United States was the most serious of the League's problems.

2. CAUSES OF WORLDWIDE DEPRESSION

A period of uneven prosperity in the decade following World War I was followed by worldwide **depression** in the 1930s. The following factors all played a part in the economic downturn:

- German war reparations
- U.S. dominance of the global economy
- High protective tariffs
- Excessive expansion of credit
- The Stock Market Crash of 1929.

The Versailles Treaty required Germany to pay reparations to the victorious powers. Since the German economy was wrecked by the war, the Germans had to borrow much of this money from banks in the United States. In addition to their effect of further draining the already impoverished Germans, the reparations also set up even more serious problems when hard times in the United States forced American bankers to call in their German loans.

The central role of U.S. production in the

During a period of hyperinflation in Germany in the 1920s, paper money was burned for fuel or used as wallpaper because it had so little value as a medium of exchange.

world economy meant that any problems experienced there would have wide consequences. In the 1920s, the United States experienced an economic boom, with a strong rise in the standard of living. American prosperity was unstable, however, and it was limited to business and industry. Farmers faced economic problems even during the best years of the 1920s. The most serious weakness in the U.S. economy was the excessive expansion of credit. Many Americans bought homes, cars, and other consumer goods on borrowed money, but some also bought stocks on credit. The good times came to an end with the 1929 Stock Market Crash, a rapid and widespread drop in the value of stocks.

When U.S. stocks lost their value, American consumers were forced to cut their spending. Industrial production slowed down, while farms continued to produce more than they could sell. To keep foreign goods out of the shrinking American markets, the government put up high tariff (import tax) barriers. Other countries did the same, cutting one another's sales and income. Around the world, severe economic depression set in.

3. TOTALITARIAN REGIMES IN THE SOVIET UNION, GERMANY, ITALY, AND JAPAN

Totalitarianism is a form of government in which a strong government tries to control all aspects of the political, economic, and social life of its people. It is kept in force through violence and is marked by a lack of freedoms for its people. Four totalitarian regimes brought misery and slaughter to their own people and others in the 1930s and 1940s.

Soviet Union. In Russia, the Communist government came to power in 1917, during World War I. Lenin soon brought totalitarian government there. After Lenin's death in 1924, his successor, Joseph Stalin, pushed totalitarianism to an extreme. Stalin strengthened both the power of the Communist state and his own personal, often arbitrary, power. His plans for the Soviet Union included an agricultural revolution to bring privately owned farms under government control. This process was called collectivization. The farms were combined into large **collective farms** (organized and controlled by the government) despite the resistance of the Soviet farmers. In the process of transforming agriculture in the 1920s, Stalin's government killed, directly or indirectly, between 5 and 10 million farmers. In the 1930s, Stalin turned his attention to **indoctrination** and terror as means of maintaining his control. He eliminated all opposition through mass arrests and murders (known collectively as the Great Purge). Another 8 to 13 million people died in this process.

In Italy, Germany, and Japan, totalitarianism had its roots in post-World War I problems including an economic depression, which

brought high unemployment, widespread bank failures, and the collapse of prices in world trading markets. The depression created popular despair and a political atmosphere in which **demagogues**, popular leaders who played on people's fears, could flourish. While the British, French, and Americans maintained their democracies, these economic problems pushed Italy, Germany, and Japan down the totalitarian path to **fascism**. (Fascism differs from communism mainly in emphasizing nationalism and in leaving most of the economy in private hands.)

Italy. World War I, in which Italy fought on the side of the victorious Allies, resulted in over 600,000 Italian lives lost. In the Versailles

Aggressive totalitarian regimes of the 1930s.

Treaty, however, Italy gained little in the way of territory. What did come to Italy after the war was severe unemployment and social unrest. In the 1920s, Benito Mussolini's Fascist party battled with Communists for political power. The Fascists won decisively, partly because Mussolini promised to restore the glory of ancient Rome. As economic conditions worsened through the 1930s, Mussolini's bold promises and forceful tactics kept him in power.

<u>Germany</u>. Adolf Hitler studied the successes of Mussolini. Germany was devastated by the economic problems of the 1920s, especially runaway inflation that made German money nearly worthless. Resentment ran high against the Versailles Treaty, especially its requirement that Germans pay reparations. Hitler played on these emotions and promised both revenge against the Jews, whom he blamed for all of Germany's problems, and a glorious future for Germany. Hitler's success in taking complete control of Germany came from his remarkable ability to exploit the fears and hopes of the German people.

It was clear that Hitler intended Germany's triumph to come at the expense of Britain and France. Because the leaders of those countries

Japanese expansionism in Asia before Pearl Harbor.

could not find an effective way to control him, Hitler was able to rebuild Germany's military forces without interference.

Japan. Until the mid-19th century, the Japanese had rejected virtually all Western influence. Then beginning in the 1850s, Japan adopted Western technology faster than any other Asian nation. This success in modernization brought both ambition and anxiety.

The Japanese wondered where they would get the raw materials to continue their industrial development. Their own islands offered little of what was needed. Still, they felt themselves to be the economic leaders of East Asia.

A group of Japanese military officers led by Hideki Tojo believed that military conquest was the only way to obtain needed raw materials and to escape economic decline. They were ready to conquer and exploit the rest of

In 1931, the Japanese invaded a part of northeast China known as Manchuria, renaming it "Manchukuo" and setting up a puppet regime there. Japan was interested in Manchuria's raw materials (coal and iron ore) and heavy industries.

East Asia to benefit Japan. As fear for Japan's future increased and worldwide depression spread, these military leaders gained control. In the early 1930s, the Japanese pursued one of their goals by invading and conquering Manchuria (in northeast China). The Japanese followed this up in 1937 with an invasion and occupation of vast parts of eastern China.

SUMMING UP

After the signing of the Versailles Treaty, one of the delegates predicted that "We are in for a high period, followed by a low period. Then there will be the devil to pay all around the world." This sums up the Interwar Period. At first, the victorious nations celebrated the end of the war. For several years, economic life in Europe seemed to be getting back to normal. In the Soviet Union, however, both economic life and everyday life were becoming less and less normal as Stalin tightened his ruthless grip on the land. Then came the worldwide economic depression, which helped two more dictators—Mussolini and Hitler—rise to power.

While Hitler carried out aggressive actions in Europe, the totalitarian government in Japan had already invaded China. Unfortunately, there seemed to be no answer to all this aggression. The British and French, determined to avoid a return to the horrors of World War I, tried to appease Hitler. Meanwhile, without the support of the United States, the League of Nations could only protest against totalitarian aggression. Thus, the stage was set for World War II.

CHAPTER REVIEW

1. Adolf Hitler became a major threat to world peace when he did all of the following *except*
   a. dismantle the democratic government in Germany.
   b. rearm Germany.
   c. fuel resentment against the Versailles Treaty.
   d. help Mussolini rise to power in Italy.

2. The *most* serious problem faced by the League of Nations was
   a. a lack of funding for international peace efforts.
   b. the absence of the United States from the organization.
   c. the unpopularity of the mandate system.
   d. British support for a Jewish homeland in Palestine.

3. All of the following factors helped to cause the worldwide economic depression of the 1930s *except*
   a. high protective tariffs.
   b. the Stock Market Crash of 1929.
   c. U.S. dominance of the global economy.
   d. totalitarian governments in Germany and Italy.

4. Before World War II, the Asian nation that was quickest to develop Western technology was
   a. Japan.
   b. China.
   c. Korea.
   d. India.

5. Which statement *best* describes totalitarian governments?
   a. Communism is the only form of totalitarian government.
   b. The governments try to control all aspects of its people's lives.
   c. These governments prove to be inefficient and generally collapse from their own weaknesses.
   d. Totalitarian governments attempt to restore past national glory.

6. The most serious failing of the Versailles Treaty was
   a. the unequal balance of power it established.
   b. its failure to include the Germans in the peace talks.
   c. its emphasis on revenge rather than peace.
   d. its failure to provide for governing Germany's colonies.

Chapter 11

World War II

Virginia Standard of Learning WHII.11

The student will demonstrate knowledge of the worldwide impact of World War II by

a. **explaining economic and political causes and major events, and by identifying major leaders of the war, with emphasis on Franklin D. Roosevelt, Harry Truman, Dwight D. Eisenhower, Douglas MacArthur, George Marshall, Winston Churchill, Joseph Stalin, Hideki Tojo, Adolf Hitler, and Hirohito.**

b. **examining the Holocaust and other examples of genocide in the 20th century.**

c. **explaining the terms of the peace, the war crimes trials, the division of Europe, plans to rebuild Germany and Japan, and the creation of international cooperative organizations.**

Standard WHII.11 a–c.
World War II and its impact

Setting the Scene

World War I (1914–1918) and World War II (1939–1945) took place so close together that they are sometimes described as two parts of one war. One of the results of the first war was creation of the conditions for the second—especially an embittered Germany, as described in Chapter 10. Another result of the first war was a change in most people's attitudes toward war. In contrast to 1914, when soldiers went off to the front in an atmosphere of excitement and adventure, most soldiers and civilians in Europe in 1939 expected the coming war to be long and terrible. They were right. World War II was the most costly conflict in history, no matter how you measure it. Sixty million people died, another 50 million were left homeless, and billions of dollars' worth of property was destroyed.

Key Questions for Standard WHII.11 a–c

1. **What were the causes and major events of World War II, and who were the leaders?**
2. **What was the Holocaust?**

3. **What other genocides took place in the 20th century?**

4. **What were the major outcomes of World War II?**

1. CAUSES, EVENTS, AND LEADERS OF WORLD WAR II

Two series of events led to World War II. One series started the war in Europe in 1939; the other led to a Japanese-Chinese war in Asia. The two fused into a global war in 1941.

War in Europe. German resentment against the Versailles Treaty paved the way for a second war in Europe. The person most responsible for dismantling the Versailles Treaty and remaking Germany as a threat in Europe was Adolf Hitler. Promising revenge on Germany's enemies, Hitler came to power in the Weimar Republic, the democratic government established in Germany after World War I. He exploited the democratic system in Germany and replaced it with a totalitarian dictatorship. He rearmed Germany. In 1938, Germany invaded Austria and pressured Britain and France into an agreement at Munich that allowed Germany to occupy part of Czechoslovakia. The British Prime Minister hoped that the Munich Agreement would preserve "peace for our time," but it did not. In 1939, Germany attacked Poland, beginning World War II in Europe. France and Britain declared war on Germany, then waited for Hitler's next move. **Appeasement**, the strategy of giving in to an aggressor's demands, had failed in the case of Nazi Germany.

Hitler's armies swept across France in 1940, forcing a French surrender. British forces in France were pushed to the sea at Dunkirk, where they were rescued by a cooperative effort of sailors and civilians. The British stood alone against Hitler, who tried to bomb them into submission. British defense of their skies, called the Battle of Britain, prevented Hitler from moving ahead with plans for an invasion. Instead, Germany and Italy attacked North Africa, then Yugoslavia and Greece. Then Germany attacked the Soviet Union. Back in 1939, Hitler had signed a treaty with Joseph Stalin, dictator of the Soviet Union, to keep the Soviets and Germans from fighting each other. In 1941, though, Hitler launched a powerful surprise attack on the Soviet Union.

War in Asia. While Hitler was rebuilding Germany for war, an aggressive government in Japan was already on the attack. The Japanese wanted industrial raw materials to build an economic empire in Asia, so in 1931 Japanese troops seized Manchuria, in northeastern China. They later occupied more of China. These were obvious cases of aggression, which the League of Nations was unable to stop. These and other events showed that the League was a failure.

Japanese expansion into Manchuria and threats toward French Indochina (now Vietnam, Cambodia, and Laos) worried Franklin Roosevelt, the U.S. President. He was further concerned in 1940 when the Japanese signed a mutual defense treaty with Germany and Italy. Then in 1941, the Japanese sent troops into Indochina, and Roosevelt responded by blocking shipments of scrap iron and aviation fuel to Japan. It was clear to the Japanese that the United States stood between them and their plans. Hideki Tojo used Japanese Emperor Hirohito as the authority for a daring strike intended to cripple the U.S. Navy. In December 1941, Tojo ordered an attack on the U.S. Pacific Fleet at Pearl Harbor. Roosevelt called the day of the attack, December 7, "a date that will live in infamy" as the United States declared war on Japan.

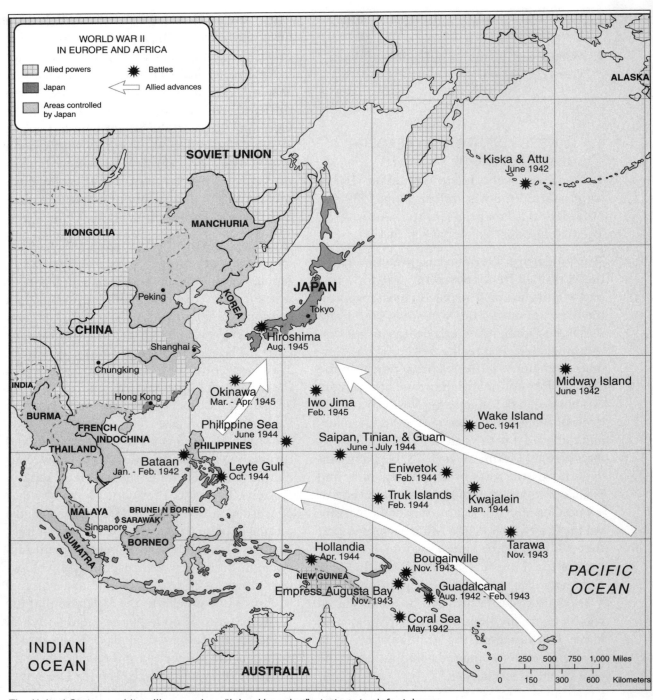

WORLD WAR II
IN EUROPE AND AFRICA

Allied powers   Battles

Japan   Allied advances

Areas controlled
by Japan

ALASKA

SOVIET UNION

Kiska & Attu
June 1942

MONGOLIA

MANCHURIA

KOREA

JAPAN

Peking

Tokyo

CHINA

Shanghai

Hiroshima
Aug. 1945

Chungking

Midway Island
June 1942

INDIA

Hong Kong

Okinawa
Mar. - Apr. 1945

Iwo Jima
Feb. 1945

BURMA

Wake Island
Dec. 1941

FRENCH
INDOCHINA

Philippine Sea
June 1944

Saipan, Tinian, & Guam
June - July 1944

THAILAND

PHILIPPINES

Bataan
Jan. - Feb. 1942

Leyte Gulf
Oct. 1944

Eniwetok
Feb. 1944

Truk Islands
Feb. 1944

Kwajalein
Jan. 1944

MALAYA

BRUNEI N BORNEO
SARAWAK

Tarawa
Nov. 1943

Singapore

BORNEO

SUMATRA

Hollandia
Apr. 1944

Bougainville
Nov. 1943

PACIFIC
OCEAN

NEW GUINEA

Guadalcanal
Aug. 1942 - Feb. 1943

Empress Augusta Bay
Nov. 1943

Coral Sea
May 1942

INDIAN
OCEAN

AUSTRALIA

0   250   500   750   1,000 Miles

0   150   300   600   Kilometers

The United States and its allies used an "island-hopping" strategy to defeat Japan.

Roosevelt had concluded long before that the United States would eventually be drawn into the war. Before Pearl Harbor, he took steps to assist the British. Most importantly, he provided war materials, especially naval destroyers, to help the British maintain their supply lines. After Pearl Harbor, the United States was at war with Japan, Germany, and Italy, which were called the *Axis Powers*. Britain, France, the Soviet Union, and the United States were the major *Allies*.

Defeat of the Axis Powers. In 1942, the U.S. Navy fought two decisive battles against the Japanese, the Battle of the Coral Sea and the Battle of Midway. Both sides suffered heavy losses. Time would show that U.S. forces could recover, but the Japanese could not. After Midway, the United States and its Allies took the offensive, driving the Japanese back toward their home islands. By the next year (1943), the war had turned against the Germans. Hitler's invasion of the Soviet Union proved a costly failure as his troops got caught in the Russian winter far from their supply lines. The Soviets held the German troops at Leningrad and Stalingrad. Meanwhile, British and U.S. forces defeated the Germans and Italians in North Africa. On June 6, 1944 ("D-Day"), Allied forces stationed in Great Britain crossed the English Channel to attack the Germans in France. Germany would be defeated as these forces moved east while the Soviet Army moved west to join them. In the Pacific, U.S. atomic bomb attacks on Hiroshima and Nagasaki contributed to the Japanese surrender.

Allied leadership. Extraordinary political and military leaders guided the British and U.S. war efforts. British Prime Minister Winston Churchill promised his people "blood, toil, tears, and sweat" as he inspired them to fight on against the Germans. He became a powerful symbol of hope for the British people. "We shall never surrender," he declared.

In the United States, President Franklin Roosevelt won re-elections in 1940 and 1944, added to his first election in 1932 and re-election in 1936. Like Churchill, Roosevelt communicated effectively with his people, maintaining their confidence and determination.

The war also produced many excellent Allied military commanders, and three of them headed the U.S. forces. General Douglas MacArthur escaped from Japanese forces in the Philippines early in the war, promising "I shall return." Later, as Supreme Allied Commander in the Pacific, he planned and led the island-hopping" campaign that defeated the Japanese army and navy. After the war, he commanded the occupation force that restored Japan's government and economy.

General Dwight D. Eisenhower commanded U.S. forces against the Germans in North Africa in 1943, then all of the D-Day invasion forces, and, after that, all Allied forces on the Western Front till the end of the war. "Ike," as he was called, was a charismatic leader and later served as U.S. President (1953–1961). Eisenhower's boss in World War II was Army Chief of Staff General George Marshall. Marshall later served as U.S. Secretary of State and Secretary of Defense and is remembered for his Marshall Plan (described on pages 128–129).

2. THE HOLOCAUST

When Hitler came to power, he used the long history of European **anti-Semitism** (hatred of the Jewish people) to his advantage. He blamed the Jews for Germany's defeat in World War I and for all of Germany's economic problems. This "scapegoating," as it is now called, was a

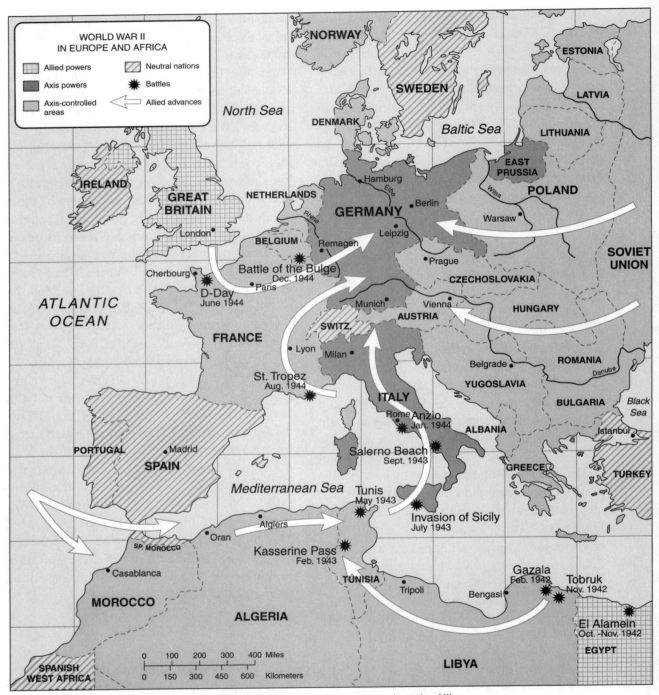

WORLD WAR II IN EUROPE AND AFRICA

Allied powers
Axis powers
Axis-controlled areas
Neutral nations
Battles
Allied advances

NORWAY
SWEDEN
ESTONIA
LATVIA
LITHUANIA
DENMARK
Baltic Sea
North Sea
EAST PRUSSIA
POLAND
Hamburg
Berlin
Warsaw
SOVIET UNION
IRELAND
GREAT BRITAIN
NETHERLANDS
GERMANY
Leipzig
Elbe
Wisla
London
BELGIUM
Remagen
Prague
Cherbourg
Battle of the Bulge
Dec. 1944
CZECHOSLOVAKIA
D-Day
June 1944
Paris
Munich
Vienna
HUNGARY
ATLANTIC OCEAN
FRANCE
SWITZ.
AUSTRIA
ROMANIA
Lyon
Milan
Belgrade
Danube
St. Tropez
Aug. 1944
ITALY
YUGOSLAVIA
Black Sea
BULGARIA
PORTUGAL
Madrid
Rome
Anzio
Jan. 1944
ALBANIA
Istanbul
SPAIN
Salerno Beach
Sept. 1943
GREECE
TURKEY
Mediterranean Sea
Tunis
May 1943
Invasion of Sicily
July 1943
Algiers
Oran
SP. MOROCCO
Kasserine Pass
Feb. 1943
Gazala
Feb. 1942
Tobruk
Nov. 1942
Casablanca
TUNISIA
Tripoli
Bengasi
El Alamein
Oct.-Nov. 1942
MOROCCO
ALGERIA
EGYPT
0 100 200 300 400 Miles
0 150 300 450 600 Kilometers
SPANISH WEST AFRICA
LIBYA

After the D-Day invasion, Germany was forced to fight a two-front war against the Allies.

way of trying to justify persecuting the Jews. Prior to his attack on Poland in 1939, Hitler's persecution of the Jews took the form of damage to property, curtailed rights, and mental and physical intimidation. The 1935 Nuremberg Laws took away the Jews' civil rights. On the *Kristallnacht* (Night of Broken Glass) in 1938, gangs attacked Jewish homes and businesses.

Once the war started, Hitler's campaign against the Jews became increasingly deadly. It spread to the conquered countries and also to other people whom Hitler declared to be inferior. For example, as German troops advanced east, they were ordered to kill Slavic peoples.

At the center of this massacre was Hitler's attempt to eliminate the whole Jewish population of Europe. This is an example of **genocide**: mass murder of a racial, ethnic, or political group. To make the killing of Jews and others more efficient, Hitler created **concentration camps**. In these camps, at least 6 million Jews were gassed or worked to death. Many were used in bizarre medical experiments. The Nazi program of mass murder also targeted the mentally ill, gypsies, homosexuals, Slavic peoples of Eastern Europe, and anyone who attempted to resist the Nazis. This was the **Holocaust**. The Nazis called it the "Final Solution."

Polish Jews of the Warsaw Ghetto were rounded up by German soldiers and sent by trains to concentration camps.

Cambodia and its neighbors.

Rwanda and surrounding African countries.

3. OTHER 20TH-CENTURY GENOCIDES

The Holocaust shocked the Allied troops who liberated its survivors and discovered the evidence of mass killing, and it continues to represent an ultimate form of inhumanity. Unfortunately, outrage over the Holocaust did not prevent other examples of genocide in the 20th century. In the most common pattern of genocide, a totalitarian government blames one of its minority population groups for all of the nation's problems, then proceeds to persecute, massacre, and attempt to eliminate that group. Here are some additional 20th-century genocides:

<u>Cambodia</u>. In 1976, Cambodian dictator Pol Pot ordered his people to abandon urban life and establish agricultural work camps across the country. The cities were forcibly emptied, and at least a million people were executed or died from starvation and disease.

<u>Rwanda</u>. During April and May of 1994, over 800,000 Rwandans were murdered, many

The lands that were formerly Yugoslavia.

chopped to pieces with machetes. The two ethnic groups of Rwanda, the Hutus and the Tutsi, had long quarreled over land, and the tension between them was accented by colonial powers in their occupation of Rwanda. Violence had erupted in 1962 when Rwanda became independent, but the events of those two months in 1994 stand out for their genocidal tragedy as extremist Hutus killed many Tutsi and drove many others out of the country as refugees. In turn, Tutsi forces killed many Hutus, resulting in a Hutu refugee problem.

Bosnia and Kosovo. Within Yugoslavia, various groups had long resented one another. Under the Communists, these resentments were submerged. When communism collapsed in Yugoslavia, however, Serbian authorities attempted the "ethnic cleansing" of Bosnian Muslims and Croats. In 1995, for example, some 6,000 Bosnians were murdered at Srebrenica (síreb-reh-NEET-sah).

In 1999, the Serbian government and its allies continued its "ethnic cleansing" in the Serbian province of Kosovo. They expelled thousands of Muslim Kosovars from their homes and murdered an undetermined number of them until massive NATO air strikes forced the Serbs to curtail their genocidal actions.

Before the Holocaust. In addition, two events that occurred *before* the Holocaust are now described as genocide. The first was the Turkish persecution of Armenians during World War I. Centuries of tension between the Muslim Turks and the Christian Armenians combined tragically with the circumstances of the war. The Turks were allied with Germany, and they feared that the Armenians would support Russia, one of Turkey's enemies in the war. The Turks forcibly deported Armenians from their homelands, and more than a million Armenians died in the process.

The second genocidal event was the killing, on Stalin's orders, of well-to-do peasants, government and military leaders, and members of the elite in the Soviet Union in the 1930s. Many

of these people were killed because Stalin saw them as rivals to his authority. The wealthier peasants, called kulaks, were killed because some of them resisted the government's seizure of their lands.

4. OUTCOMES OF THE WAR, NEW WORLD LEADERS, NATO, THE WARSAW PACT, AND THE UNITED NATIONS

Decline of European imperialism. As World War I had done earlier, World War II raised nationalistic hopes in Asia. Japanese victories over European forces in Asia, though later reversed by U.S. victories, had a great psychological effect in undermining European imperialism. The Japanese had proved that Europeans were not invincible.

World War II raised nationalistic hopes in Africa also. In African colonies where the white population was small, as in British West Africa, independence tended to come peacefully. However, where large numbers of Europeans had moved into a colony, the result was violence, as in French Algeria and British Kenya. The British and French were reluctant to accept the possibility of losing their empires, but at the same time they had limited economic and military resources to invest in keeping them. After 1945, the question was not *whether* Asian and African colonies would become independent but when. (See the map on the next page.)

Two major world powers. Only one major nation came out of World War II clearly better off than when it went in. That was the United States. War production overcame the problems of the Great Depression, and science gave the United States the atomic bomb. The Soviet Union came out of the war as a great power too (despite the loss of at least 20 million people)

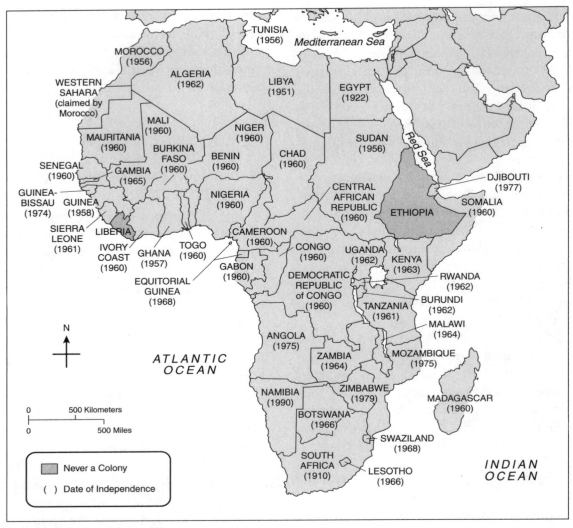

Colonial independence in Africa.

and, after a couple of years, would develop atomic bombs also.

Military opposition to Soviet communism was organized by the creation of the North Atlantic Treaty Organization (NATO), in 1949. NATO allied the United States with Canada and most of the nations of Western Europe for the collective defense of its members against possible Communist aggression. In response, the Soviet Union created an alliance with its "puppet states" of Eastern Europe. This was called the Warsaw Pact, created in 1955.

Recovery in Germany and Japan. Both Germany and Japan showed remarkable powers of recovery after the war and today are leading industrial powers, but the approaches taken for assisting the two nations differed sharply. The Germans were occupied by four victorious nations, while only the United States occupied Japan. Because the Allies feared that Nazism was still strong in Germany, they banned Allied soldiers from mixing with German civilians in social activities. No such ban was applied to Japan. The most unique feature of the occupation of Japan was the writing of a new Japanese constitution that declared "the Japanese people forever renounce war. . . . Land, sea, and air forces, as well as other war potential, will never be maintained." The United States, it was agreed, would guarantee Japan's security.

War crimes trials. One decision all of the victorious powers agreed on was that the perpetrators of the Nazi Holocaust and other war crimes should be tried and punished. A War Crimes Tribunal set up in the city of Nuremberg, Germany, brought 22 Nazi leaders to trial for a range of "crimes against humanity." Twelve were sentenced to death. Later, more Nazis were tried for their crimes.

The Tokyo Trials were less publicized than the Nuremberg Trials. In Tokyo, General MacArthur brought 25 Japanese war leaders to trial for atrocities, especially ones against the Chinese. Seven were sentenced to hang and 16 to life imprisonment. Historians have questioned whether the Tokyo trials went far enough to punish the many serious offenses committed by Japanese soldiers during the war. One thing is certain, though: MacArthur focused U.S. resources on helping the Japanese people regain their economic strength and national self-confidence, not on punishment.

The United Nations. The nations fighting against the fascist powers started calling themselves the "United Nations" in 1942. This alliance of nations was the source of the idea for an international organization by the same name, the United Nations or UN. In 1945, 50 nations signed the UN charter, which, it was hoped, was a far better plan for an international organization than the League of Nations had been. The strongest arm of the UN was the Security Council, composed of the United States, Great Britain, the Soviet Union, France, and China. The UN does a wide range of humanitarian work and has nearly 200 members. The UN's efforts to settle international disputes have met with limited success.

SUMMING UP

In World War II, the totalitarian governments of Germany, Italy, and Japan attempted to dominate the rest of the world. Some historians say they almost succeeded, but in the end, the Allies proved too strong in soldiers and war materials. The strongest of the Allies, the United States and the Soviet Union, assumed world leadership at the war's end, which was also the end of their alliance. Quickly, new alliances developed—NATO around the United States and the Warsaw Pact around the Soviet Union. In this process, Europe was divided between communism and democracy.

The upheavals of World War II encouraged movements for liberation from colonial rule around the world and led to the rise of new African and Asian nations. Also, like World War I, World War II created conditions for bitter future conflicts. In Chapter 12, you will read about the cold war between the United States and the Soviet Union and about "hot wars" in Asia.

CHAPTER REVIEW

1. Japanese aggression of the 1930s and 1940s was most directly linked to
   a. fear of China.
   b. need for raw materials.
   c. U.S. threats to Japan.
   d. opposition to British colonialism.

2. Hitler's most costly defeats came as a result of his
   a. occupation of North Africa.
   b. alliance with Japan.
   c. air war over Britain.
   d. invasion of the Soviet Union.

3. Which statement *best* describes the results of the battles of Coral Sea and Midway?
   a. After these two defeats the Japanese were unable to continue fighting.
   b. Both sides suffered heavy losses, and while the United States could recover, the Japanese could not.
   c. These costly "draws" had little impact, and it was the atomic bomb that the turned the tide against the Japanese.
   d. After these battles, the Japanese controlled much more of the Pacific Ocean.

4. Which leader is *not* correctly matched with his words?
   a. Churchill—"blood, toil, tears, and sweat"
   b. Roosevelt—"a date that will live in infamy"
   c. MacArthur—"I shall return."
   d. Stalin—"peace for our time"

5. The commander of Allied forces for the D-Day invasion was
   a. MacArthur.
   b. Churchill.
   c. Marshall.
   d. Eisenhower.

6. The collapse of communism in Yugoslavia is directly connected to which genocide?
   a. murder of Jews by the Nazis
   b. the killing of kulaks on Stalin's orders
   c. "ethnic cleansing" of Muslims by Serbs
   d. the killing of former government officials, members of minority groups, and others by Pol Pot

ERA VIII

The Postwar Period, 1945 to the Present

12

The Cold War

Virginia Standard of Learning WHII.12

The student will demonstrate knowledge of major events and outcomes of the cold war by

a. **explaining key events of the cold war, including the competition between the American and Soviet economic and political systems and the causes of the collapse of communism in the Soviet Union and Eastern Europe.**

b. **assessing the impact of nuclear weapons on patterns of conflict and cooperation since 1945.**

c. **describing conflicts and revolutionary movements in East Asia, including those in China and Vietnam, and their major leaders, i.e., Mao Tse-tung (Zedong), Chiang Kai-shek, and Ho Chi Minh.**

Standard WHII.12 a, b. The cold war: key events and the role of nuclear weapons

Setting the Scene

Wartime conferences of the Allied leaders, especially one held at Yalta in 1945, gave Stalin the go-ahead to retake Russian territories lost in World War I, but the Soviets actually took much more. Soviet forces that had liberated Eastern Europe from Nazi Germany simply stayed on to impose Soviet control.

Winston Churchill called this the descent of "an iron curtain." Behind the curtain in Eastern Europe, Soviet-controlled governments were estab-lished, agriculture was reorganized on the Soviet model, and all opposition to the Soviets was ruth-lessly eliminated. At this time, only one Eastern European nation defied the Soviets. In Yugoslavia, Marshall Tito created a Communist dictatorship that followed its own nationalist course. Mean-while, the Soviet and U.S. governments grew in-creasingly suspicious of each other's motives.

With the defeat of Germany, the major Allies (Britain, France, the USSR, and the United States) divided Germany into four zones of occupation, which were to work together economically. The So-viet Union, however, kept its zone separate, so in 1949 the country was divided into West Germany under the three Western Allies and East Germany under the Soviet Union. The city of Berlin was then also divided into two parts. The problem of Germany demonstrated the lack of trust and rising hostility between the Soviets and the democracies. When the Soviet Union developed the atomic bomb in 1949, conditions were right for a tense stand-off between the United States and its allies on the one hand and the Soviet Union and its **satellite nations** on the other. This was the **cold war**.

Key Questions for WHII.12 a, b.

1. **How did atomic weapons influence international relations from 1945 on?**
2. **What events brought the United States and the Soviet Union into conflict?**
3. **How did the cold war affect Asia?**

1. THE ATOMIC AGE

Atomic weapons were created in the United States during World War II and were ready for use in August 1945. Germany had also started an atomic weapon project but had surrendered in May before completing it. As U.S. forces pressed closer to Japan in bloody battles, President Harry S. Truman (Franklin D. Roosevelt had died in April) ordered the dropping of atomic bombs on two Japanese cities, Hiroshima and Nagasaki. Despite criticism of the use of such devastating weapons, Truman judged at the time that it would save months of war and countless thousands of lives.

After World War II, concerned Americans and others raised the possibility that a third world war involving atomic weapons would be even more terrible than the first and second, perhaps even fatal to the whole human race. At the same time, U.S. leaders attempted to apply a lesson of World War II—that hostile nations should not be "appeased." Giving in to Hitler's demands in the 1930s, for example,

had not stopped his drive for conquest. Now U.S. leaders were determined to face off against Communist aggression with overwhelming military strength—an approach that would bring immense risks. Atomic weapons (and the later, more powerful weapons using nuclear fusion) gave the United States the means to carry out this policy.

The strategy of **deterrence** was the opposite of appeasement. Deterrence meant that the United States was able and prepared to respond to any Soviet nuclear attack with an equally destructive strike. Since an attack would result in "mutually assured destruction" (both sides certain to be destroyed), it would therefore never be made. That, at least, was the theory, but many people were concerned about an accidental or unauthorized nuclear strike or a strike ordered by a crazed head of state. They compared the two world powers to two men in a gasoline-filled room threatening each other with matches. Fortunately, the strategy of deterrence did work, preventing any direct war between the United States and the Soviet Union.

2. CONFLICTS BETWEEN THE UNITED STATES AND THE SOVIET UNION

The Truman Doctrine. In 1947, the United States and Great Britain were worried about possible Communist takeovers of Greece and Turkey. The British were no longer able to exert power in the eastern Mediterranean, so President Truman committed the United States to support (with $400 million) the economies and the military organizations of Greece and Turkey. This Truman Doctrine made it less likely that Communists would be able to take control of those countries.

The Marshall Plan. Soon the United States followed with an aid program intended to help all of Europe rebuild from the war. It was announced by Secretary of State George Marshall and came to be called the Marshall Plan. Since Stalin turned down aid to the Communist nations of Eastern Europe, the Marshall Plan aided only Western European countries, including former enemies of the United States—Germany and Italy. West Germany's rapid economic rebirth demonstrated the plan's effectiveness and was in contrast to the economy of Communist East Germany, which suffered serious and long-lasting economic problems.

The Berlin Wall. After Stalin died in 1953, Nikita Khrushchev (khroosh-CHOV) emerged from a power struggle as the leader of the Soviet Union (1958–1964). To stop a steady flow of refugees fleeing to the West from Communist Eastern Europe, Khrushchev in 1961 decided to close the last remaining hole in the iron curtain—the border between East and West Berlin. He ordered the building of a wall between the two halves of the city. When completed, this Berlin Wall hindered East Germans from fleeing to Western Europe. The United States protested the building of the wall but took little action against it.

The Cuban Missile Crisis. Khrushchev took a more dangerous step in 1962. The Soviets began building nuclear missile sites on the island of Cuba, which had become a Communist country headed by Fidel Castro in 1959. U.S. intelligence sources told President Kennedy about the missiles in 1962, and he demanded that they be

In 1948 and 1949, during the Berlin Conflict, Allied transport planes such as this one flew supplies into Berlin. The Soviet Union had cut off ground transport routes between Berlin and the West.

dismantled and removed. U.S. naval vessels set up a **quarantine** (forced isolation) of Cuba to prevent the Soviets from bringing any more weapons to that island nation only 90 miles from the United States. People around the world saw that nuclear war was a real possibility. After negotiations, however, Khrushchev agreed to dismantle the missile sites and remove the missiles. Kennedy gained, and Khrushchev lost, considerable prestige from this dangerous confrontation. Other Soviet leaders accused Khrushchev of misjudging the young U.S. President, while Americans praised Kennedy for choosing a firm but moderate response to the crisis. The two leaders soon set up a "hot line" between Washington, D.C., and Moscow to help head off any future crises.

3.   THE COLD WAR IN ASIA

What did the cold-war years mean for the world outside the United States and Europe? The United States and the Soviet Union viewed other continents in terms of possible gains and losses for democracy or communism. They fought the cold war by trying to gain the support of the newly independent nations. Asia, the most populous continent, was a particularly crucial cold-war battleground. Some Asian nations, including South Korea, Taiwan, and Israel, lined up on the side of the United States. Others sought the support of the Soviets. Many, such as India, attempted to remain neutral.

For the United States, any spread of communism seemed dangerous. For this reason, Truman and his successors followed a policy of **containment**, which is like a quarantine to stop the spread of disease. This policy had worked in Western Europe, as discussed above. Containment took the form of regional alliances and, in Korea and Vietnam, a willingness to commit troops against perceived Communist aggression. Against this backdrop of great-power confrontation, leaders of the newly independent countries sought national security and economic development.

4.   THE END OF THE COLD WAR

Communism collapsed in the late 1980s and early 1990s. Explanations are numerous, but certainly Eastern Europeans were tired of the rule of fear under communism. Growing nationalism undermined the unity of the Warsaw Pact. Eastern European nations were also frustrated with the poor performance of Communist economies. The Soviet Union's economy was failing too. In Soviet towns and cities during the 1980s, long lines formed to get small amounts of food, and many goods were traded on the "black market" (unofficial or illegal channels). In 1986, a nuclear disaster at Chernobyl in Ukraine further hampered the Soviet economy, in addition to taking hundreds of lives.

Soviet General Secretary Mikhail Gorbachev (Gor-ba-CHOV) recognized the popular frustration in Eastern Europe and the Soviet Union, and he carried out reforms. Meanwhile, U.S. President Ronald Reagan kept strong military, political, and economic pressure on the Soviet leaders. In 1987, for example, he challenged Gorbachev to "tear down this wall" in Berlin. Two years later, Gorbachev let the East Germans know that Soviet soldiers would no longer be used to hold the two Germanies apart, and the Berliners took the wall down. Soon Germany would be reunified.

Then in 1991, some of Gorbachev's Communist opponents tried to stem the collapse of the Soviet Union by staging a coup. Even though their plan failed (partly because of street demonstrations against the coup leaders), Gorbachev soon resigned. Then the Soviet Congress of Deputies transferred all of its powers to the individual republics of the former union, and the Soviet Union was no more.

Russia remained a world power, however, with a deadly arsenal of nuclear weapons. Largely out of concern about those weapons, the United States treated Russia cautiously. NATO, however, expanded in the late 1990s despite Russian opposition. In 1999, Poland, the Czech Republic, and Hungary became members, and other nations are expected to join in later years.

A West German pounds away at the Berlin Wall. Built in 1961 by the East German government to prevent its citizens from escaping, the wall symbolized a divided Germany. In 1989, German citizens forced the wall to be opened; a year later, East and West Germany were united as one country.

Standard WHII.12 c.
Revolutionary movements in Asia

Setting the Scene

In Asia, pro-Communist and anti-imperialist movements came together in explosive ways. To many policy-makers in the United States, Asian communism seemed to be a direct extension of Soviet communism, but the reality was far more complicated than that. Within a few years of the end of World War II, Communist China emerged as the third major world power alongside the United States and the Soviet Union, and Korea and Vietnam became sites where the cold war turned into a hot war.

Key Questions for WHII.12 c

1. **How did Mao Zedong come to power in China?**

2. **What caused the Korean and Vietnam conflicts?**

1. MAO ZEDONG

In 1927, a civil war began in China. It pitted the Nationalists led by Chiang Kai-shek against the Communists led by Mao Zedong. The year 1934 was especially difficult for the Communists, as they had to flee the Nationalists in a "Long March" of 6,000 miles though southern and western China over the course of a year. This perilous escape made Mao a legendary figure and kept the Communist force intact. Two years later, Chiang Kai-shek and the Communists agreed to stop fighting each other and formed an alliance to fight against the Japanese, who had invaded northern China (Manchuria).

When Japan surrendered in 1945, the Chinese civil war started up again, and this time the Communists won decisively. Mao became the ruler of the People's Republic of China in 1949. The losers in the civil war established a Chinese government in exile on the island of Taiwan, where they have had economic success despite the fear of invasion by mainland Chinese.

For the People's Republic of China, the 1950s and the 1960s were years of dramatic and costly changes. In the 1950s, Mao forced the peasants into agricultural collectives, a move that produced a massive famine. At the same time, Mao demanded that the Chinese produce large quantities of steel and manufactured goods in their backyards. Fearing a U.S. invasion, he ordered heavy industries located on the coast to be moved west into the country's interior. In the 1960s, Mao's Red Guard, an army of young people, terrorized the Chinese people and prevented opposition to his government. Mao died in 1976, but even a few years before that China began moving toward stronger economic ties with Western nations. Private enterprise has been reintroduced into the Chinese economy. A slower movement toward political freedoms, however, has been punctuated by outbreaks of repression. The Communist party remains in power in China.

2. THE KOREAN AND VIETNAM CONFLICTS

Korean conflict. After World War II, two Korean nations developed, much as Germany had been divided in Europe. There was an industrial, Communist north and a rural, non-Communist south. When North Korea invaded South Korea in 1950, President Truman committed U.S. forces, under United Nations authority, to defend South Korea. Early U.S. successes were undone by a massive attack by Chinese forces aiding North Korea. U.S. troops

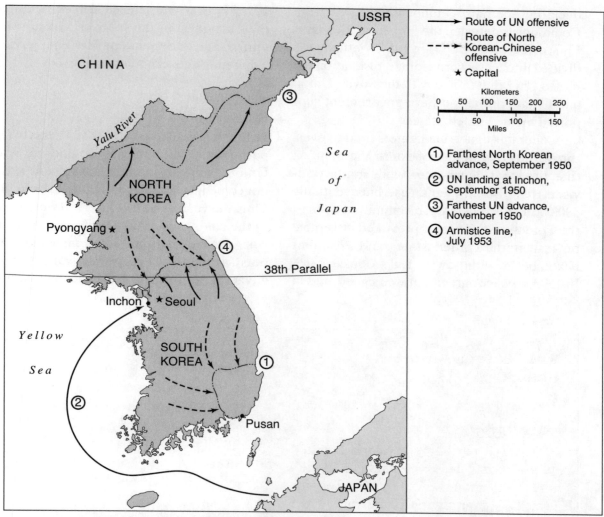

A divided Korea and events during the Korean War.

regained the offensive, and their commander, General MacArthur, sought to expand the war into Communist China. To avoid such a larger war, President Truman relieved MacArthur of his command. In 1953, North and South Korea signed an armistice, leaving Korea divided along virtually the same line that had existed prior to the war—the 38th parallel. The United States considered the war a success because it prevented a Communist takeover of South Korea. Since the end of the war, South Korea has industrialized and prospered, while North Korea has suffered severe economic difficulties.

Vietnam conflict. At the end of World War II, Ho Chi Minh (hoh chee MIN), the major Vietnamese Communist leader, triggered a long war for independence against the French by declaring Vietnam's independence. After the Communists defeated the French at Dien Bien Phu (díyen-bíyen-FOO) in 1954, Vietnam was divided into a northern Communist nation led by Ho Chi Minh (allied with the Soviet Union and China) and a southern government supported by the United States.

Communist guerrilla fighters tried to overthrow the government of South Vietnam. At first, the U.S. role was to provide military advisers to the South Vietnamese, but eventually 500,000 U.S. soldiers were committed to fight the Communists. The war provoked disruptive protests in the United States, and President Nixon began withdrawing U.S. troops in 1969. In 1973, a peace agreement was signed, and in 1975, North Vietnamese forces completed their conquest of the south. The result was a united and independent Vietnam under a Communist government.

SUMMING UP

In the period after World War II, the two superpowers, the United States and the Soviet Union, faced off in mutual suspicion but did not come into armed conflict with each other. Thus, the years from 1945 to 1990 were known as the cold-war period. During this time, new rules for international relations were developed, as the two superpowers sought to gain advantages through their influence on other

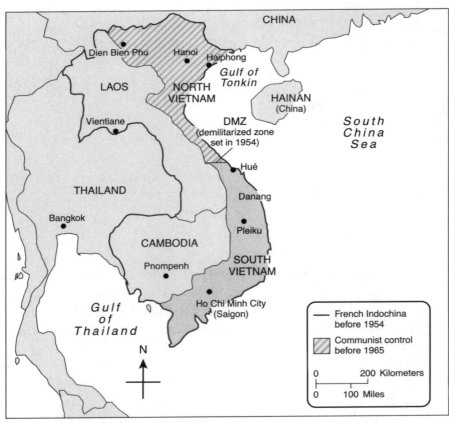

Southeast Asia during the war in Vietnam.

The Cold War / 135

nations. The cold war often benefited these nations, since economic aid was an important part of their relationship with the superpowers. Occasionally, however, the superpower rivalry produced bloody regional conflicts. By the end of the century, the cold war had ended, the Soviet Union had fallen apart, and the United States stood as the single superpower.

CHAPTER REVIEW

1. The World War II conference of Allied leaders held at Yalta is most often associated with
   a. Soviet control of Eastern Europe.
   b. German recovery.
   c. the ending of the Pacific War.
   d. the development of the atomic bomb.

2. At the end of World War II, Germany and the city of Berlin were both divided, with the eastern sector of each being controlled by
   a. France.
   b. Britain.
   c. the United States.
   d. the Soviet Union.

3. The outcome of the Cuban Missile Crisis was
   a. the strengthening of the Soviet military presence in Cuba.
   b. the dismantling of missile sites and removal of missiles from Cuba.
   c. war between Cuba and the United States.
   d. the loss of United States prestige in the region.

4. The U.S. President who challenged Gorbachev to tear down the Berlin Wall was
   a. Bill Clinton.
   b. George Bush.
   c. Harry Truman.
   d. Ronald Reagan.

5. The Chinese Civil War was interrupted in 1937 as the Nationalists and Communists joined forces against the
   a. Americans.
   b. British and French.
   c. Soviets.
   d. Japanese.

6. Which statement comparing the Korean and Vietnam conflicts is *not* true?
   a. In both cases, Communist forces fought non-Communist ones.
   b. Neither war resulted in complete victory of Communist forces.
   c. The bulk of the fighting against the Communists in both wars was done by the United States.
   d. In each case the northern state fought against the southern state, with the United States supporting the southern one.

Chapter 13

Independence Movements

Virginia Standard of Learning WHII.13

The student will demonstrate knowledge of political, economic, social, and cultural aspects of independence movements and development efforts by

a. **describing the struggles for self-rule, including Gandhi's leadership in India.**

b. **describing Africa's achievement of independence, including Kenyatta's leadership of Kenya.**

c. **describing the end of the mandate system and the creation of states in the Middle East.**

Standard WHII.13 a. Struggles for self-rule: focus on India

Setting the Scene

At the end of World War I, the defeated nations lost their colonies. After World War II, the victorious nations gave up their colonies, though not very willingly and not all at once. Instead, Asian and African colonies demanded independence and found ways to pressure the colonial powers in that direction. The circumstances of each case differed. Some independence efforts were violent, while others were not.

The first big change came in India. When World War II ended in 1945, it was clear that the British would not continue to rule India for much longer. The Labour party that had come to power in Britain was opposed to colonialism, while in India an extraordinary leader named Mohandas Gandhi led the independence movement.

Key Questions for Standard WHII.13 a

1. **How did Gandhi lead India to independence from colonial rule?**

2. **What were the results of the Indian independence movement?**

1. HOW GANDHI LED INDIA TO INDEPENDENCE

Two issues dominated Indian politics at the end of World War II. The first was the question of Indian independence from the British. The second was the concern of India's Muslims over their place in an independent India dominated by Hindus. An organization called the Muslim League campaigned for a separate Muslim nation on the grounds that Muslims feared discrimination in a Hindu India. It became clear to many that India would have to be **partitioned** (divided into separate parts) between Muslims and Hindus. The last British **viceroy** (governor) of India, Lord Mountbatten, carried out a plan for India to become independent in 1947 and for a Muslim state of Pakistan to be created.

It is unlikely that the British would have granted India its independence in 1947 if it had not been for the nonviolent resistance movement led by Mohandas Gandhi, a spiritual leader. Gandhi had led protests against British rule even before World War I. That war further stimulated Indian sentiment for freedom. Indian troops fought hard for the British in the war, but the British continued to view India as a necessary part of their empire. It took many years of pressure from Gandhi and other leaders to bring the British to serious consideration of Indian independence. World War II shifted British opinion further toward independence for India. This fact was reflected in the election of a Labour party government in Britain to replace the pro-empire Conservative party of Winston Churchill. The Labour party favored Indian independence.

Mohandas Gandhi (center) led a march to the sea in 1930 to protest a British monopoly on salt in India.

South Asia today.

2. RESULTS OF INDIAN INDEPENDENCE

The agreement that established independence for India in 1947 also established Pakistan, a Muslim nation made up of two parts, one northeast and one northwest of India. One year later, the large island off the southeast coast of India—then called Ceylon by the British—also became independent. Renamed Sri Lanka in 1972, this island nation has been troubled by a long-standing conflict between its government and the Tamil minority group, who are fighting to establish an independent state.

The creation of India and Pakistan led to mass disruptions and migrations, as many Hindus in Pakistan moved to India while many Muslims in India moved to Pakistan. Deadly clashes frequently broke out between the two groups. A Hindu who was distraught over the partition assassinated Gandhi in 1948. In 1971, another division in the area took place when the eastern section of Pakistan became the independent country of Bangladesh.

India proved that a successful democracy could be built in a country with a huge population and widespread poverty. Unfortunately, tensions between India and Pakistan have continued into the 21st century.

Standard WHII.13 b.
Independence movements in Africa

Setting the Scene

As in Asia, independence movements flourished in Africa after World War II (see map on page 122). In 1946, Egypt, Liberia, Ethiopia, and South Africa were the only sovereign states in Africa. But over the next several decades, many independent African countries were formed. In the course of only one year, 1960, 16 African states became independent. Now there are 53 nations in Africa.

Europeans' rationale for having colonies was attacked in the postwar period. The Charter of the United Nations guaranteed colonial populations the right to self-determination, and the UN consistently took stands against colonialism and racism. Africans felt increasingly strong nationalism, pride in African cultures and heritage, and resentment over colonial exploitation.

Key Questions for Standard WHII.13 b

1. **Why did African independence movements gain success after World War II?**
2. **What role did Jomo Kenyatta play in Kenyan independence?**

1. AFRICAN INDEPENDENCE MOVEMENTS

African independence efforts followed three general patterns. The first pattern was peaceful transition to independence. This was common in colonies that had only small European populations and minimal tension among the African groups within the colony. In those colonies, of which Ghana in British West Africa was a good example, the colonial power's job was straightforward—to identify the people who would assume power and then make plans for turning the colony over to them.

The second pattern was one of violent transition to independence, or violence following the transition, due to conflicts among Africans. Nigeria was an early example. In Nigeria, independence was delayed by complicated negotiations among African ethnic groups, and independence led quickly to civil war. The boundaries for African nations followed the colonial boundaries that Europeans had drawn, often without regard for the views of the African groups involved. Thus, it is not surprising that independence alone could not satisfy everyone's nationalistic ambitions.

A third pattern developed where large European populations had settled in the colony, as in Algeria, Kenya (discussed on the next page), and South Africa. These colonies faced three-sided conflicts, in which the European settlers resisted both the desires of native populations and a colonial power's plans to establish African majority rule. For years in Algeria, the French simply refused to consider independence. According to French law, Algeria was legally a part of France, as Hawaii is of the United States today. In fact, Algeria was so highly valued that other French colonies, including Tunisia and Morocco, were given independence to allow French forces to concentrate on keeping Algeria. Finally in 1962, following a war that had killed thousands of French soldiers and hundreds of thousands of Algerians, the country gained independence.

South Africa, the country with the largest white population in Africa, achieved independence after World War II, but by 1948 the South African government made separation of the races, called **apartheid** (uh-PAR-teht), the nation's policy. Nelson Mandela led the struggle against apartheid, which was finally overcome in the 1990s.

2. KENYA

In 1945, Kenya's European population had significant economic and political power, though it made up less than 1 percent of the nation's population. The European settlers owned the best farmland, and they expected to keep their privileged position when independence came. Having been active in the African independence movement since the 1920s, Jomo Kenyatta (JOH-moh ken-YAH-tah) became the recognized leader of the independence movement in Kenya. Kenyatta sought to win African control of the country through a gradual process. His efforts were interrupted by an uprising of radical African nationalists. This "Mau Mau (MAH-oo MAH-oo) uprising" was put down by the British after four years of fighting, in which about 70 Europeans and 18,000 black Africans were killed. Protesting his innocence, Kenyatta was put in jail in 1953 on charges of leading the Mau Mau uprisings.

In the next decade, the British government decided not to continue its support of the European minority in Kenya. Kenyatta was released from jail in 1961, and in 1963 he became the Prime Minister of an independent Kenya. Kenyatta wisely put economic development as the new country's top priority and encouraged European settlers to stay. He did not want the country to lose such a large pool of skilled workers, entrepreneurs, and managers all at once. Kenyatta encouraged investment in his country, and many foreigners did invest in this politically stable, solidly anti-Communist new country. Until the mid-1970s, Kenya's economy ran well despite the fact that the country had only one political party. The one-party system produced corruption, which grew worse after Kenyatta's death in 1978.

Standard WHII.13 c. New states in the Middle East

Setting the Scene

At the same time that India was being divided into India and Pakistan, British-controlled Palestine was also divided. Unlike India, Palestine came under British control not as a colony but as a mandate, a territory moving toward independence. As in India, partition failed to control violent conflicts in Palestine.

Key Question for Standard WHII.13 c

How were new states created in the Middle East after World War II?

NEW STATES IN THE MIDDLE EAST

Nationalism dominated political affairs in the Middle East after World War II. This nationalism was a complex mix of religious belief, ethnic identity, and anti-Western feelings. After the former mandates Jordan, Lebanon, and Syria became independent nations, some Middle East leaders sought to build a union of independent Arab nations strong enough to resist the influence of Europe and the United States. Unfortunately for the advocates of this union, the artificial boundaries drawn up for these states had never been completely acceptable to the people who lived there. Unity among Arab nations has been achieved only in their common resistance to a Jewish state in Palestine.

During World War I, the British government pledged to support a Jewish homeland in Palestine. In the 1930s, **Zionism**, the movement to establish a Jewish homeland, gained momentum from Hitler's persecution of the Jews in Europe. Suddenly, there were many thousands of Jews who wanted to escape Hitler's actions by moving to Palestine. This boost in the numbers of Jewish immigrants to Palestine created a reaction among the Muslims who lived there. How could a home be created for one group of people when another group already lived there? The only answer seemed to be dividing the land between Palestinians and Jews. In 1948, the Jewish part became the independent state of Israel. It soon successfully defended itself against attacks by Egypt, Syria, Lebanon, and Iraq. Resistance to Israel became a common bond among the other Middle East nations, and three additional Middle East wars have been fought over the Arab-Israel conflict.

SUMMING UP

Former colonial possessions in East Asia, Southeast Asia, Africa, and the Middle East gained independence after World War II. For these new states, unity and prosperity proved challenging. Achieving independence rarely meant an end to conflict.

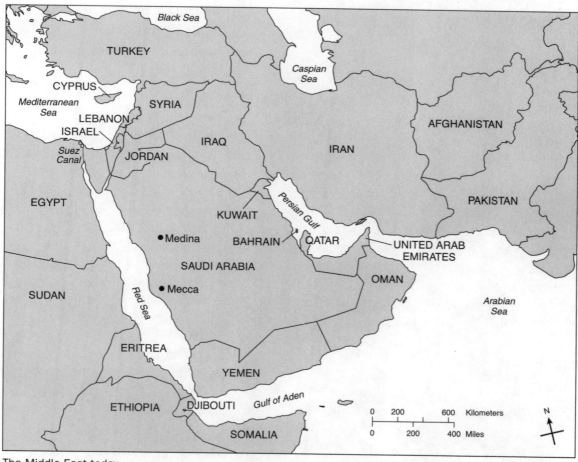

The Middle East today.

CHAPTER REVIEW

1. India was partitioned at independence as a result of
   a. disagreements between Gandhi and the British government.
   b. conflict between Hindus and Muslims.
   c. differences between British and French colonial policies.
   d. the effects of World War II.

2. The dominant influence on politics in the Middle East after World War II was
   a. Zionism.
   b. communism.
   c. nationalism.
   d. poverty.

3. The most violent African war of independence took place in
   a. Kenya.
   b. Nigeria.
   c. Ghana.
   d. Algeria.

4. The United Nations Charter made a strong statement against
   a. apartheid.
   b. colonialism.
   c. nationalism.
   d. communism.

5. Jomo Kenyatta's government of Kenya was most successful in
   a. providing free and open elections.
   b. building a modern military.
   c. avoiding corruption.
   d. economic development.

Chapter

14

Major Religions in the Contemporary World

Virginia Standard of Learning WHII.14

The student will demonstrate knowledge of the influence of Judaism, Christianity, Islam, Buddhism, and Hinduism in the contemporary world by

a. describing their beliefs, sacred writings, traditions, and customs.

b. locating the geographic distribution of religions in the contemporary world.

In this chapter, each of the five major religions is discussed separately in terms of the topics of Standard WHII.14 a, b. At the end of this chapter, the information is summed up in a chart so that you can compare the religions across these topics.

Standard WHII.14 a, b. Five major religions: their history and their role in the world today

Setting the Scene

Religion has formed the basis for civilizations for thousands of years. Indeed, the ethical, moral, and spiritual foundations of the world's cultures have come from the **tenets** (basic principles) and beliefs of religion. Five religions have dominated the major cultures and civilizations of the world: Judaism, Christianity, Islam, Hinduism, and Buddhism. Much of history is told in terms of the leaders and the important events to be found in those five major religions.

Discussion of religion in the popular media might convey the impression that religion is in decline in the modern world. Actually, despite the development of modern nonreligious philosophies and worldviews, the five major religions combined have more followers today than at any time in history.

Key Questions for Standard WHII.14 a, b

1. **What historical events help to define each religion?**

2. **What are the religion's major beliefs, sacred writings, traditions, and customs?**

3. **What is the distribution of the religion's followers throughout the world?**

4. **What are some of the ways the religion influences other activities and beliefs?**

Judaism

1. HISTORY

The religion of the ancient Hebrews is known today as Judaism. Abraham was the first great leader of the Hebrews and is described as the founder of the tribe. Jews believe that God made a **covenant** (agreement) with Abraham, making them God's "chosen people." The Hebrews migrated to Egypt, where they were enslaved. Their next great leader, Moses, freed them from slavery by taking them out of Egypt.

The Jews returned to Palestine, the "Promised Land" that they believed God intended for them. There they established the kingdom of Israel. Under the rule of King Solomon in the 10th century B.C., Israel thrived, as demonstrated by its extensive trade, military strength, and architecture, particularly the great temple of Jerusalem. To this day, Jerusalem is the most important holy city of the Jews. After Solomon's death, the kingdom disintegrated.

In A.D. 135, under the rule of the Roman empire, the Jews were driven out of Palestine and dispersed. This event is called the **Diaspora**. Jews were scattered from India to Spain. In most of their new homes, Jews suffered prejudice called anti-Semitism. During the first half of the 20th century, anti-Semitism grew to be a dominant theme in the speeches and policies of several European leaders, above all Germany's Adolf Hitler. Under Hitler's rule (1933–1945), millions of European Jews were killed in what has come to be called the Holocaust (see page 119).

2. BELIEFS, SACRED WRITINGS, TRADITIONS, AND CUSTOMS

The Hebrews recorded their earliest history in the Torah, which is divided into five books (Genesis, Exodus, Leviticus, Numbers, and Deuteronomy). These books also make up the beginning of the Old Testament in the Christian Bible. They tell of the beginning of the Jewish religion with Abraham, describe the exile in Egypt, and relate how Moses won freedom for the Hebrews. They say that God made a covenant with Moses on Mount Sinai, decreeing how the Jews were to worship and to live an ethical and just life by following the Ten Commandments.

Unlike most of the religions of the time, early Judaism taught that there was one all-powerful God. Belief in one god is called **monotheism**. (Belief in more than one god is called **polytheism**.) In addition, Judaism teaches that God will send a Messiah, one anointed by God to unite the Jewish people and lead them in God's way.

Jewish Holy days include Passover, which celebrates the escape from slavery in Egypt. Jews also celebrate each 24-hour period from Friday evening until Saturday evening. This is the Sabbath, or holy day of the week. The holiest day of the Jewish year is the Day of Atonement, or Yom Kippur (YOHM kee-POOR). This day is a day for expressing one's regrets for past bad deeds and hopes for performing good deeds in the coming year.

Jews worship in synagogues, where part of each service includes reading from the Torah. Many Jews follow traditional rules that dictate or define actions in their daily lives. For example, there are strict dietary rules that prohibit the eating of certain foods and the preparation of different types of food with the same utensils and containers.

3. GEOGRAPHIC DISTRIBUTION

Judaism was founded in Judea (Palestine) and is now practiced mostly in North America, Europe, and Israel.

4. INFLUENCES ON CONTEMPORARY LIFE

The influence of Jewish thought and beliefs is to be found throughout the history of Western philosophy and religion. Both Christianity and Islam are based on the books of the Torah and revere Abraham and Moses. Principles of Jewish law have been especially important in Europe and the United States, including the ideas that "no man is above the law" and that "sons cannot be punished for the sins of the fathers."

Christianity

1. HISTORY

Christianity has its roots in Judaism. During the time that Palestine was controlled by the Roman empire, Jews there believed that God would send them a Messiah, a great leader who would free them and establish the kingdom of God on earth. Jesus of Nazareth was a Jewish carpenter who began preaching to large crowds about salvation and its reward—eternal life. Much of what he said came from Jewish beliefs about ethical behavior and followed the Ten Commandments. In addition, Jesus declared himself to be the Messiah and the Son of God. (He is also known as the Christ, which like Messiah means the anointed one.) He turned from the traditionally Jewish belief of an eye for an eye, and instead preached mercy and forgiveness.

Jesus and his **disciples** (followers) were the founders of Christianity. When Jesus started to preach to the people of Judea, many people at first supported him as the Messiah. Some Jews, however, resented his growing influence. Roman authorities sought political advantage by putting Jesus to death. He was nailed to a cross and left to die, a brutal form of execution called **crucifixion**. Christians believe that Jesus was resurrected three days after his death, and that he visited his disciples and commanded them to continue his teaching.

Christianity spread rapidly through the Roman empire as its advocates, such as the Apostle Paul, became missionaries, preaching Christian beliefs to Jews and non-Jews alike. The Romans at first tolerated Christianity, but they later came to associate it with rebellion against Roman rule and brutally persecuted the Christians. This continued until A.D. 313, when the Emperor Constantine, who had converted to Christianity, stopped the persecution.

Despite persecution, the early Christian church grew. As the western part of the Roman empire declined, the Christians, who had been organized as the Roman Catholic Church, became the dominant social and political force in Western Europe. In order to meet the challenges of this expanded role, Catholic Church councils set up new religious doctrines and practices.

In Eastern Europe, the Christians became organized as the Eastern Orthodox Church. Over the next thousand years, this two-way split continued. In the 16th century, the Protestant Reformation split Christianity in Western Europe into numerous churches and faiths (see Chapter 3).

2. BELIEFS, SACRED WRITINGS, TRADITIONS, AND CUSTOMS

The Old Testament of the Hebrews together with the New Testament of Jesus's teachings make up the Bible, the holy text of Christianity.

Bethlehem (where Jesus was born) and Jerusalem (where Jesus was tried and crucified) are holy cities. Christmas (which celebrates the birth of Jesus) and Easter (which celebrates his resurrection) are the most important holy days, and Sunday is the day of worship. The central belief is that there is one God and Jesus is the Son of God. Salvation will be achieved only by faith and good works.

3. GEOGRAPHIC DISTRIBUTION

Christianity, like Judaism, was founded in Judea (Palestine). It later spread to all continents by European migration and colonization, as well as by missionaries. It is concentrated in Europe and North and South America.

4. INFLUENCES ON CONTEMPORARY LIFE

Christianity is the world's largest religion. At one time, it was the state religion for all the European nations, so much of European culture and tradition is based on the Christian faith. The Roman Catholic Church had great power and influence throughout the Middle Ages and into modern times. Most medieval art is Christian in terms of subject matter. There are countless paintings of Jesus and his mother Mary, of the saints (holy men and women), and of biblical scenes such as Jesus's crucifixion.

Islam

1. HISTORY

The founder of Islam was Muhammad. Muhammad was an Arab merchant in Mecca (also spelled Makkah) who proclaimed that there was one true God called Allah. In A.D. 622, he and his supporters went to the city of Medina (also spelled Madinah). This journey is called the **Hegira** (hee-JY-ruh). At Medina, Muhammad became a political, religious, and military leader. He captured Mecca and united much of the Arabian Peninsula under Islam. After Muhammad's death, Islam was ruled by four of his followers known as **caliphs** (KAY-lifs), all of whom were powerful and capable leaders. When the last of the four, Ali, was murdered, a power struggle developed that came to be called the Sunni/Shi'a split. The Sunni won the larger following, but the Shi'a sect has survived to the present day as the more traditional form of Islam.

2. BELIEFS, SACRED WRITINGS, TRADITIONS, AND CUSTOMS

The Qur'an (koo-RAHN: also spelled Koran) is the Muslims' most important holy text. They believe that Allah (God) dictated the text to Muhammad, who in turn dictated it to several scribes.

The holy cities of Islam are Medina and Mecca, both in today's Saudi Arabia. The Five Pillars of Islam are a Muslim's five basic duties: (1) declaring one's faith, (2) praying daily, (3) giving to the poor, (4) fasting from sunrise to sunset during the holy month of Ramadan, and (5) at least once during one's life making the **hajj**—a pilgrimage to Mecca.

The Muslim holy days are the month of Ramadan, which is devoted to fasting and prayer. (Ramadan moves from year to year on the Western calendar.) Five times every day, Muslim men stop what they are doing and pray, facing Mecca. Muslim services are held in **mosques**. The Qur'an is not translated into other languages for Muslims whose language is not Arabic. Instead, all Muslims learn Ara-

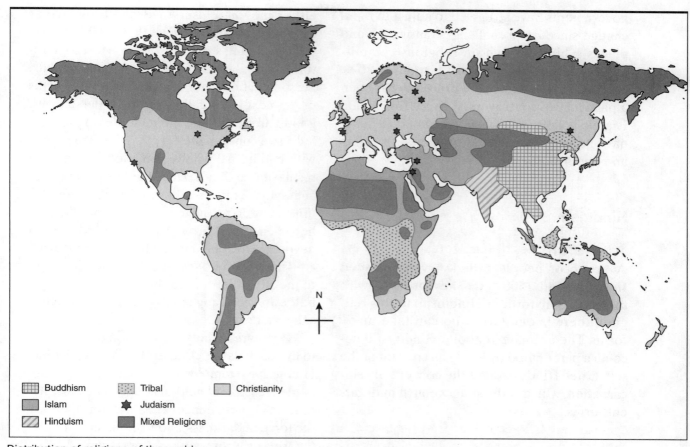

Distribution of religions of the world.

bic in order to read and study the Qur'an. The Muslim holy day of the week is Friday.

The most important beliefs of Islam are that there is one God, Allah, and that Muhammad is his prophet. If a Muslim follows the laws of the Five Pillars, he or she will reach salvation. Islam takes its roots from both Judaism and Christianity, including all of the Hebrew prophets. Like Judaism and Christianity, it reveres Abraham and Moses. It differs from Christianity in that Muslims do not believe that Jesus was the Son of God, though they do believe he was an important prophet.

3. GEOGRAPHICAL DISTRIBUTION

By A.D. 800, Muslims had conquered much of the Middle East and North Africa. Today, Islam is the leading religion throughout the Middle East and much of Africa and Asia.

4. INFLUENCES ON CONTEMPORARY LIFE

The ideal government for many Muslims is a **theocracy**, a nation run according to religious principles, specifically those of the Qur'an. In this ideal theocracy, all people would be equal before God. Some of the real-life Islamic governments have struggled to adjust to rapid change, since Islam challenges innovation and places a higher value on religious commitments than on government responsibilities. The proper role of women in society has been a particularly controversial issue. Traditional Islamic beliefs have been associated, in some nations, with restrictions on women's rights and opportunities.

Hinduism

1. HISTORY

A group of people called Aryans invaded India around 1500 B.C. They brought with them an early form of Hinduism. In this religion, there is one God who can take many forms. The ultimate goal of a Hindu is to become a part of God by losing all concept of the self. Later Hindus added the concept of **reincarnation**, which is the soul's rebirth in different forms.

2. BELIEFS, SACRED WRITINGS, TRADITIONS, AND CUSTOMS

In Hinduism, there is no single sacred text, such as the Torah, the Bible, or the Qur'an. The beliefs of the Hindus were recorded in collections called the Vedas (VEH-duz) and the Upanishads (yoo-PAN-uh-shads). These are the most important religious texts to the Hindus.

Hindus believe that there is one all-powerful force in the universe, which they call Brahma. Because Brahma is profoundly complex, the belief in this one fundamental deity can take the form of worshipping gods and goddesses that represent certain aspects of it. The Hindu goal is to achieve a state of oneness with Brahma. Hindus believe that all actions have consequences, and that actions result in

either moving closer to Brahma or farther away. Hindus also believe that until a person has attained this state, he or she is forced to return and live another life. The sum total of all a person's actions that determine the level of his or her next life is called **karma**. A person with good karma will live the next life on a higher level as a consequence of good deeds; a person with bad karma will live on a lower level as a result of bad deeds. Thus, Hindus believe that achieving Brahma takes more than one lifetime. They do not have priests, but they do have holy men, called **gurus**, who provide advice and devote their lives to meditation and prayer.

There is no holy city, but many Hindus go to the city of Benares in India, where they can bathe in the Ganges River, which they consider sacred.

There are no holy days, although the goal is to live each day as close to Brahma as possible. Hindus have temples, where they can meditate in the presence of helpful images. The most significant of these images are Shiva, representing the force of darkness, and Vishnu, representing the force of preserving and protecting.

3. GEOGRAPHIC DISTRIBUTION

Hinduism was founded in India and is still centered there.

4. INFLUENCES ON CONTEMPORARY LIFE

Hinduism led to a strict division of social classes called the **caste system**. Traditionally, Hindus believe that the only way to move up in this system is to lead a good life and hope to be reincarnated into a higher caste. The highest caste is called the Brahmin, and Brahmins are believed to be one step away from becoming part of God. The caste system has made it very dif-

Religion and Origin	Major Leaders and Events	Sacred Writings	Traditions, Customs, and Beliefs	Mono-/ Poly- theistic	Geographic Distribution Today	Political/ Social/ Economic Influence
Judaism Began in Palestine around 2000 B.C.	Founded by Abraham and Moses; the Diaspora; the Holocaust; the creation of modern Israel	The Torah	God made a covenant with the Jews as the Chosen People; emphasis on the teachings of the first five books of the Hebrew Bible, called the Torah; dietary laws; synagogue services; non-proselytizing, ethnic religion;	One God	North America, Israel, Europe	"No man above the Law"; the Ten Commandments
Christianity Began in Palestine, A.D. 30	Founded by Jesus of Nazareth, Saints Peter and Paul; Roman Catholic Church; Reformation; Eastern Orthodox Church; Martin Luther, John Calvin	Bible (Old Testament and New Testament)	Belief in Jesus as the Son of God; salvation by faith and good works; proselytizing—sent out missionaries to spread Christianity and convert nonbelievers	One God	All continents	Catholic Church influenced rise of European states; religion spread as part of Western European colonialism; supported the rise of capitalism
Islam Began in Arabia, A.D. 622	Founded by the Prophet Muhammad; Hegira; Sunni and Shi'a; Madinah, Makkah	Qur'an	Five Pillars—faith, prayer, charity, fasting, and the hajj (pilgrimage); salvation by a just life of belief in the one true God; proselytizing	One God	Africa, Asia	Some governments based on principles of the Qur'an
Hinduism Prehistoric India	Founded by ancient Aryans	Vedas, Upanishads	Reincarnation; karma; Brahma-Vishnu-Shiva; gurus; nonproselytizing, ethnic	Polytheistic: one God has many forms	Asia	Caste system organizes people into fixed classes
Buddhism 563 B.C.	Founded by Siddhartha Gautama; nirvana; Zen	No sacred text	Enlightenment; sacredness of all life; detachment from worldly desires; Four Noble Truths; Eightfold Path; proselytizing	Neither	Asia	Nonviolence

ficult for people with ability and talents to achieve success outside their prescribed places and roles. These limitations have been breaking down, however, under pressure from the Indian government. As with Islam, traditional Hinduism has been most controversial in its effects on the treatment of women.

Buddhism

1. HISTORY

Buddha (meaning "the enlightened one") was the title given to Siddhartha Gautama (sid-DAR-tuh GAH-oo-tuh-muh). He was born in India around 563 B.C. and gained thousands of followers by teaching others how to reach enlightenment. After Buddha's death, missionaries spread his beliefs across Asia. One of the major periods of missionary activity was during the reign of the Emperor Asoka, who is remembered both for his enthusiastic promotion of Buddhism and his tolerance of other faiths. Despite the efforts of Asoka, Buddhism eventually faded in India. In Japan and North America, a form called Zen Buddhism has been especially popular. It is associated with quiet meditation and attaining peace of mind.

2. BELIEFS, SACRED WRITINGS, TRADITIONS, AND CUSTOMS

The Tripitaka (tree-PIT-uh-kuh) is the collection of Buddha's sermons and commentaries.

Buddha preached the Four Noble Truths: (1) all life is full of suffering, (2) suffering is caused by desire for things, (3) suffering can be overcome by giving up desire, and (4) desire can be overcome by following a set of strict rules. These rules are called the Eightfold Path, which requires that one accept the Four Noble Truths, do good, meditate, and practice moral and ethical behavior. By following the Eightfold Path, the Buddhist can become enlightened and eventually reach **nirvana**—a state of oneness with the universe. Unlike heaven, which is a place, nirvana is the ultimate state of mind. Buddhists do not believe in a personal god.

3. GEOGRAPHIC DISTRIBUTION

Buddhism began in India but virtually died out there. It is concentrated today in East Asia and Southeast Asia.

4. INFLUENCES ON CONTEMPORARY LIFE

Buddhism rejects the caste system of Hinduism and preaches nonviolence. In the modern world, Buddhism has promoted a vegetarian lifestyle and a thoughtful detachment from worldly concerns. It has also been a factor in political conflict, notably in the relations between China's Communist government and Buddhist Tibet.

SUMMING UP

The table on the previous page summarizes the basic features of Judaism, Christianity, Islam, Buddhism, and Hinduism. The listings include the key terms you should know.

CHAPTER REVIEW

1. Which of the following religions could be considered a polytheistic religion?
   a. Islam
   b. Judaism
   c. Christianity
   d. Hinduism

2. Believing in the Five Pillars of Wisdom would be characteristic of what faith?

   a. Islam

   b. Judaism

   c. Buddhism

   d. Christianity

3. Hindus believe in the idea of

   a. observing many holy days.

   b. reincarnation.

   c. a pilgrimage to Mecca.

   d. the son of God.

4. Christianity and Islam shared a similar development in that they both

   a. had an internal power struggle that split them into two major factions.

   b. had difficulty in converting other peoples to their faith.

   c. evolved into major polytheistic faiths.

   d. accepted the Eightfold Path to Enlightenment.

5. Muslim and Hindu teachings have historically had a limiting effect on

   a. travel and exploration.

   b. architectural advances.

   c. women's rights.

   d. higher education.

6. In the Torah, you find the major sacred writings of what religion?

   a. Islam

   b. Buddhism

   c. Judaism

   d. Hinduism

Chapter

15

Contemporary Issues

Virginia Standard of Learning WHII.15

The student will demonstrate knowledge of cultural, economic, and social conditions in the developed and developing nations of the contemporary world by

a.   **identifying contemporary political issues, with emphasis on migrations of refugees and others, ethnic/religious conflicts, and the impact of technology, including chemical and biological technologies.**

b.   **assessing the impact of economic development and global population growth on the environment and society, including an understanding of the links between economic and political freedom.**

c.   **describing economic interdependence, including the rise of multinational corporations, international organizations, and trade agreements.**

Standard WHII.15 a.
Contemporary political issues

Setting the Scene

As the world crossed over into the 21st century, several 20th-century problems hung on. Ethnic and religious conflicts smoldered in much of the world but broke into armed conflict most often in the world's poorer countries. Lack of resources for a decent life, or the unfair distribution of those resources, contributed to the violence, and violence produced refugees seeking to escape.

Key Questions for Standard WHII.15 a

1.   **Why have so many people become refugees?**

2.   **What ethnic and religious problems continue to trouble the contemporary world?**

3.   **How have new technologies created opportunities and problems?**

1. REFUGEES AND IMMIGRANTS

The many small wars of the 1990s drove the number of **refugees** (people forced to flee their homeland) worldwide to 40 million, compared to fewer than 3 million in 1960. Europe in the 1990s became a source of refugees for the first time since the 1940s, as a result of fighting among Serbs, Bosnians, and Croats.

War has not been the only cause of disruption. Poverty has played a large part too. The primary reason for immigration, legal and illegal, into Europe and the United States has been to find work. After leaving their homelands to escape poverty, many immigrants have faced racism and discrimination. For examples, Hispanic immigrants to the United States and North African "guest workers" in European cities have both faced these burdens.

Some Western Europeans and Americans have felt overwhelmed by the number of new people who differ in language, culture, and religion from their own. Large refugee populations will continue to raise tensions in some parts of the world. At no time in history have more people been uprooted from their homes.

2. ETHNIC AND RELIGIOUS PROBLEMS

The Arab-Israel conflict. Religious faith has long been a focus for conflict in the Middle East. The Christian Crusades (1096–1291), for example, were campaigns to retake the Holy Lands from Muslim rulers there. Since its founding in 1948, the nation of Israel has often been at war with neighboring Arab countries and some Palestinians living and/or working in Israel. Though

Displaced Ethiopians waited for food distribution in the town of Adi Gudom. Hundreds of thousands of Ethiopians had fled hostilities between Eritrea and Ethiopia in 1998.

religion was the critical issue in the creation of Israel, the Arab-Israel conflict is also one of shortages—too little land and water to accommodate both the Palestinians and the Israelis. The many years of violence have built barriers too, as each side has developed a deep distrust of the other. Palestinian acts of terrorism have been met with Israeli military retaliation, followed by further terrorism and retaliation in a tragic cycle.

As a result of the Arab-Israeli War of 1948, about 700,000 Palestinian Arabs became refugees. Today, the number of Palestinians living outside of Israel is some 2.5 million. While most of them have settled comfortably in neighboring Arab countries and elsewhere, many thousands still live in refugee camps outside Israel. Most Palestinians await the time when a Palestinian state might be set up in the area. The assassination, by a Jewish extremist, of Israeli Prime Minister Yitzhak Rabin in 1995 was a major setback for the region. Rabin had accepted the idea of a Palestinian state and was prepared to negotiate with the Palestinian leaders. His assassination inflamed political differences among Israelis, and his successors have not been as willing to compromise with the Palestinians. For the foreseeable future, Palestinian refugees will continue to seek land, citizenship, and freedom. The Israelis will continue to defend their right to exist as a nation.

Northern Ireland. Ireland is a Roman Catholic country that was occupied by English forces in the 16th century. The Irish were never comfortable under English rule, in part because wealthy English people took ownership of much Irish land. Moreover, Irish Catholics could not vote, hold office, or inherit or purchase land. After years of protests, in 1921 most of Ireland (except the northern part) declared itself free from Britain.

The Protestant majority in Northern Ireland wanted that area to remain part of Great Britain, which is predominantly Protestant. The Catholic minority in the north, though, wanted the area to join with the rest of Ireland. Ever since, violence has broken out repeatedly between Irish Catholics and Protestants in Northern Ireland over such issues as job discrimination, police brutality, and the political status of the area.

Between 1968 and 1998, Northern Ireland was devastated by acts of terror, including bombings and assassinations. Much of the violence was attributed to the Irish Republican Army (IRA), which wants to force Northern Ireland into a unified Ireland. In 1994, however, the IRA declared a cease-fire, and a peace agreement followed in 1998. The agreement could not wipe out distrust, especially among extremists on both sides, and the peace was shaky. Catholic and Protestant church leaders have condemned violence as a means to resolve the conflict. The British government continues to seek a fair and lasting resolution of the issues, but the situation remains a dangerous one.

3. NEW TECHNOLOGIES

Technology advanced at a lightning pace in the 1990s, particularly in computers, communications, and biology. Development of more powerful computers in smaller sizes has revolutionized most jobs. Huge ships and aircraft are now designed on computer screens. Complex surgeries are directed from long distances. Ordinary people are in touch with vast sources of information, available any time of the day on the Internet. How well this information surplus will be used remains to be seen, but what has been said of the railroad, the steamship, and the airplane—that the world has been made smaller—is certainly true of the Internet also. Also true of the Internet is an old saying that "the rich get richer and the poor get poorer." Worldwide acess to computers and instantaneous communications is extremely unequal. In 2000, about 60 percent of the U.S. population regularly used the Internet and about 35 percent in South Korea. By contrast, only 6 percent of the people in Brazil, and an even smaller percentage in Nigeria had regular Internet access.

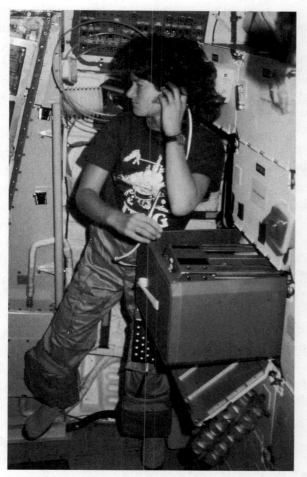

In 1983, Sally Rider became the first female U.S. astronaut to go into space. She is shown aboard the space shuttle *Challenger*.

Dangerous technologies have come into more hands too. Just as the end of the cold war in 1991 did not end all conflicts, neither did it end the hazards posed by nuclear weapons. These weapons have proliferated (spread) to a number of nations including India, Pakistan, and Israel. Nuclear weapons projects in Iran and North Korea are a cause for concern, as these countries might strike at us or at our allies. Also terrorist groups might obtain and use (or threaten to use) nuclear weapons on us or our allies. Chemical and biological weapons are also a threat in the 21st century, a point illustrated by a Japanese religious group's poison gas attack on the Tokyo subway system in 1995.

On the positive side, huge numbers of new products and devices have been created to make one's work easier or to provide entertainment. For example, it is possible to enjoy movies and music almost anywhere using DVD and compact disk players. New inventions have made life more comfortable and enjoyable for most people in the developed countries, and have reached some people in the developing countries too.

New medical procedures and drugs cure or relieve a variety of illnesses, but even as technology has improved the quality and length of life, it has created difficult choices. The Internet speeds medical information among doctors, hospitals, and insurance companies, but how is individual privacy to be protected if anyone can find out your medical history?

Medical science can prolong life, but should it always do so? Scientists, for example, can modify genetic codes to eliminate biological defects, but what unforeseen side effects could this have on human genes?

Manned space exploration has had some dramatic successes, but are the successes worth the costs? What other scientific goals (or more general goals of society, for that matter) have been sacrificed to make manned space exploration happen? Could not unmanned space flights accomplish the same goals at less cost?

Pessimists say that technology is moving too fast for sound judgment to guide it and that the consequences will be disastrous. Optimists acknowledge that new technologies bring new problems, but they believe that people will continue to solve the problems that arise or at least find a way to adjust to them.

Standard WHII.15 b. Economic development and population growth

Setting the Scene

The world is divided into the developed and the developing nations, with some nations dangling in between. Developing nations are those that continue to struggle with geographic and historical problems on their way to modern economic success. The developing nations include many African, Asian, and Latin American nations. These nations lack modern industrial and agricultural technology. Their people often lack access to modern education and effective medical care.

While the developing world is plagued by poverty, the developed world enjoys impressive, though unevenly distributed, wealth. A number of countries, including the former Communist countries of Eastern Europe, occupy a place between these two worlds of poverty and wealth. These countries are much better off than the developing countries of sub-Saharan Africa, for example, but their people still face limited economic opportunities.

Key Questions for WHII.15 b

1. **What problems do developing nations face?**
2. **How has rapid economic development affected the environment?**

1. PROBLEMS OF DEVELOPING NATIONS

During the cold war, the United States and the Soviet Union provided economic aid to developing nations in hopes of gaining their support. With the end of the cold war came the end of much of this aid. Nations need money to modernize, and the developing nations have borrowed money from the World Bank and the International Monetary Fund, as well as from other sources. Many developing nations have been unable to repay these loans.

Population growth rates are high in developing countries, and increasing population causes the wealth of the country to be spread more and more thinly among its people. Some countries are actually experiencing reduced wealth per capita (per person) each year. Fears that population growth would cause worldwide famine have lessened as food production has made major advances. Hunger and illness continue to affect the developing nations, however. Cholera, yellow fever, and measles continue to devastate some parts of Africa and the Americas. AIDS, the acquired immune deficiency syndrome, is an especially serious threat in Africa but is also a major problem in parts of Asia. Many additional public health problems result from the rapid growth of cities, which can overwhelm available resources and services.

One service that is inadequate in many developing countries is public education. As a result, illiteracy will continue to limit job opportunities in those countries. Through modern communications, developed nations have become aware of the suffering in developing nations, but awareness has not produced the amount of help that is needed in Africa, some parts of Asia, and in Central and South America.

2. ECONOMIC DEVELOPMENT AND THE ENVIRONMENT

One of the most influential and frightening books of the 1960s, Rachel Carson's *Silent Spring*, continues to have a prominent place on bookstore shelves in the 21st century. Carson warned that pesticides sprayed on crops (including DDT) were killing birds, fish, and animals, and building up in people's bodies. The environment was being poisoned.

In some places, the environment is also being destroyed. In the Amazon region of South America, the tropical rain forests are being cut down for farmland. Species of plants and animals are disappearing forever as their habitats are being destroyed. The environment is undermined in other ways, such as the use of gases in aerosol cans and refrigerators that damage the ozone layer above the earth. The damaged ozone layer cannot protect against harmful effects of ultraviolet rays from the sun, which cause cancers. Also serious is the buildup of carbon dioxide in the atmosphere, from cars and factories. This buildup may cause devastating climatic changes over time.

Some environmental hazards of development are not hidden. Acid rain, which contains sulfur from factory exhaust, has killed huge patches of forest in North America and Europe. Oil tankers have run aground, releasing deadly oil into the ocean. Nuclear power plants have leaked radiation. In 1984, toxic fumes from an explosion at a chemical plant in India killed 2,000 people.

Rachel Carson died in 1964, just two years after the publication of her landmark book. Eight years later, Congress passed a law banning the use of DDT.

Standard WHII.15 c. Economic interdependence

Setting the Scene

From space, astronauts can see what is sometimes not obvious here on earth—that all of the world's people are "in the same boat." In that distant view, the land masses shrink in size and national boundaries become invisible. Indeed, the countries of the world are increasingly dependent on one another for raw materials, markets, and financial resources. This is called economic interdependence.

Key Question for WHII.15 c

How are national economies interdependent?

The developed and developing countries are linked together by patterns of trade, loans, and foreign aid. They are also linked by **multinational corporations** (business firms that operate in multiple countries). The multinational corporations can put large amounts of money into research for new products, can choose the best locations for manufacturing these products, and can market their products all over the world.

Many multinational corporations began in the United States, and as they spread consumer products around the world, American popular culture is often exported too. Critics of this process call it "coca-colonization," but the picture of U.S. goods assailing foreign markets is oversimplified. Japanese corporations manufacture many of their products, especially automobiles, in the United States and Mexico. In point of fact, automobiles rarely come from any one country. They are examples of international cooperation, with parts from different countries that are assembled in still others.

Nations have grouped together for economic strength also. One of the most successful groups is the European Union, which has encouraged economic cooperation by eliminating trade barriers. In 1992, the Treaty on European Union committed the European nations to establishing a common currency, the euro, which has been adopted by 12 member nations.

The World Trade Organization (WTO) was formed to set up wide-ranging rules for international trade. The WTO has encouraged greater access to markets and increased international trade. Their successes in these matters have

Anti-WTO demonstrations, such as this one in the Philippines in 2001, are efforts to protest trade rules which many people in developing countries think are unfair.

been accompanied by controversy over the effects of WTO rules on nations' labor and environment laws. Often the rules override such laws, resulting in fewer labor rights and poorer environmental standards, claim the critics.

Interest in a trade agreement for North America led Canada, Mexico, and the United States to create the North American Free Trade Agreement (NAFTA) in the early 1990s. This is working toward a single market, without trade barriers, of more than 420 million people.

SUMMING UP

Technology and commerce link the nations and individuals of the contemporary world in ways that were inconceivable just a short time ago, before the dangerous cold war ended. There is a genuine prospect of world peace and prosperity as the 21st century begins. Unfortunately, numerous religious, racial, economic, and ethnic disputes; crushing poverty in developing nations; millions of refugees with nowhere to go; and a wide range of threats to the natural environment complicate this hopeful picture.

CHAPTER REVIEW

1. Which statement best describes the refugee problem now?
   a. Refugees are a tragic circumstance, but modern nations have shown a consistent willingness to take in most people dispossessed by war.
   b. Refugees have become relatively few since the end of the cold war.
   c. Many small wars have produced some 40 million refugees with nowhere to go.
   d. Negotiations have usually resolved refugee problems that arise from racial and ethnic conflicts.

2. Which of the following does *not* apply to both the Arab-Israeli and Northern Ireland conflicts?
   a. religious differences
   b. a cycle of violence
   c. deep distrust on both sides
   d. conflict beginning in the period after World War I

3. How has the end of the cold war affected aid to developing countries?
   a. Without the motive of the cold war, Russia and the United States have been less willing to provide aid.
   b. Aid to Africa and Asia continues at the same level as at the height of the cold war.
   c. The economies of developing countries have improved so much that they need little aid.
   d. The end of cold-war military expenses has enabled the United States to significantly increase its aid to developing countries.

4. Which of the following does not correctly pair a cause with its effect?
   a. forest destruction—species extinction
   b. aerosol gases—damaged ozone layer
   c. pesticides—climatic changes
   d. factory exhaust—acid rain

5. The World Trade Organization (WTO) has contributed to economic development by
   a. opening markets to businesses around the world.
   b. supporting organized labor.
   c. protecting the environment.
   d. making loans to developing countries.

Glossary

CHAPTER 1

artifact—any human-made object from the past. Artifacts such as pottery, weapons, and the ruins of buildings can provide information about the way people lived.

cultural diffusion—the spread of customs, ideas, foods, etc., as people of one culture meet people of another culture

indigenous—native, or belonging naturally to a place

monsoon—a wind over South Asia and the Indian Ocean that changes direction according to the time of year. The southwest monsoon of May to October brings heavy rain to the land.

natural resources—materials in the environment that humans can use, such as water, soil, metal ores, and petroleum

physical maps—ones that emphasize natural features of land and water

political maps—ones that emphasize human-made features, such as national borders and cities

primary sources—historical records, such as documents and artifacts, that date from and belong to the time being studied

projection—in map making, a means of recording the curved surface of the earth on a flat piece of paper. Different projections are used for different purposes. For example, one projection may show distances accurately but not areas; another projection may show areas accurately but not distances.

secondary sources—historical writings dating from a time later than the one being studied

typhoon—a severe windstorm that occurs over the Pacific Ocean

CHAPTER 2

humanism—a new outlook on life that arose during the Renaissance, inspired partly by ancient Greek and Roman writings. Humanists believed that each human is unique and has great worth.

principality—a state ruled by a prince. Russia and Germany are nations that were once groups of principalities.

CHAPTER 3

capital—money that is used to produce more money or to start a business. A **capitalist** is a person who uses money these ways. **Capitalism** is the economic system in which goods and services are produced using the capital of individual investors.

divine right of kings—a belief that the monarch is God's representative, and therefore his or her decisions must not be challenged

heretic—a member of a religion who rejects that religion's doctrine, or basic beliefs. This rejection is called **heresy**.

indulgence—in the medieval Church, a pardon that could be purchased

investment—putting money into a project or fund in hopes that it will return more money

liturgy—the form of worship in a religion or religious sect

missionary—a priest or minister who preaches in a distant area or foreign country and attempts to convert people to his or her religion

penance—a punishment, such as the saying of many prayers, set by a priest for sins heard at confession

predestination—in general, the belief that people have no real choice in what they do—that free will is an illusion; in particular, the Calvinist belief that God already knows who will be saved and will be damned, and that one's actions will not affect the outcome

simony—the practice of buying a position as priest

usury—the charging of interest on loans

CHAPTER 4

absolute rule—a political system in which orders come from the top down, with no questioning

cash crop—an agricultural product that is grown for sale, not for the farmer's own use

colony—in general, a group of people from one country who settle in another area. Most often the group takes power over any people already living there and develops the colony for the benefit of the country they came from.

Columbian Exchange—the carrying across the Atlantic of crops, animals, technology, and culture previously unknown on the other side

conquistador—Spanish for "conqueror"; one of the Spanish military leaders in charge of taking over lands and peoples in the Americas

hereditary—passed down from parent to child

mestizo—a person who has both European and Native-American ancestors

plantation—a large farm on which cash crops are grown and most of the workers live

triangular trade system—a pattern of trade that developed across the Atlantic Ocean after European colonization of the Americans. In one triangle, slaves were carried from Africa to the Americas and traded for raw materials (such as cotton and sugar). These were carried to Europe and traded for manufactured goods (such as guns or rum). Then these were carried to Africa and traded for slaves.

CHAPTER 5

joint-stock company—a type of business (pioneered by the Dutch) that raised money from a group of investors, each of whom would contribute a share of the total and then receive a share of any profits. This was the forerunner of today's corporation.

mercantilism—the prevailing economic theory of the late Middle Ages and after that a country's wealth and power depended on acquiring as much gold and silver as possible from its overseas **colonies**, and, in turn, on selling its manufactured goods to its colonists

samurai—the warrior class of ancient Japan. The samurai supported the **shogunate**.

shogunate—a system of military government, headed by a **shogun**, or general, that rose to power in medieval Japan

CHAPTER 6

absolute monarchy—a government in which one person (the monarch) has total or near total control of the nation's financial resources and laws

authoritarian—demanding strict obedience

Baroque period—the 17th and early 18th centuries when the arts, especially music and architecture, tended to complexity and showiness

Bill of Rights—a set of statements outlining rights of all citizens

bourgeoisie—the French term for the middle class

bureaucracy—a body of nonelected government officials with set rules and a strict line of authority from the top down

Classical period—in music, the late 18th and 19th centuries, when musical pieces emphasized clarity, balance, and moderation

commission—a group of people set up by a government either to investigate an issue or to oversee an activity

commoners—people who were not part of the nobility

constitutional monarchy—system of government in which the monarch's powers are limited and the real power is in the hands of an elected parliament. In today's constitutional monarchies, such as Britain and Norway, the monarch has virtually no governing power.

coup d'état—seizure of power by force

ellipse—an oval outline, like a circle with bulges on opposite sides. Whereas every point on a circle is the same distance from its center, every point on an ellipse is the same total distance from two "centers."

enlightened despotism—the reign of an **absolute monarch** who believes that he or she is using his or her power for beneficial (good) purposes

estate—social class

experimentation—the process of testing ideas or claims under controlled conditions, a central feature of modern science

habeas corpus—the first words in a Latin phrase describing the right of people not to be imprisoned without a trial

heliocentric—with the sun at the center. The heliocentric model of the solar system replaced the belief that the sun revolved around the earth.

heresy—a belief that is counter to the official doctrine of a religion

rationalism—the philosophical view that that reason is superior to faith

taille—a tax formerly levied by a French king or lord on his subjects or on lands held of him

CHAPTER 7

annex (verb)—to take over neighboring land, usually by force or the threat of force

balance of power—the near equality of power among nations (or between two sets of nations), with the idea that this will discourage open aggression by any of the nations involved

conservative—in politics, generally favoring tradition, cautious and gradual change, and respect for authority

ideology—the set of ideas that make up the political program of a party or the political outlook of an individual

industrialization—the development and spread of power-driven machinery and the factory system

liberalism—a political view that generally favors change over tradition in such matters as civil and political rights

Napoleonic Code—a system of laws set up by Napoleon Bonaparte after the French Revolution. It still forms the basis of French laws.

nationalism—belief that people who share the same language, culture, and ethnic background belong together in the same state. Nationalism also applies to the belief that one's nation is as good as or better than others.

realpolitik—German for the politics of reality, the belief that politics should be based not on theories or ethics but on whatever works best to benefit one's nation

urbanization—the growth of cities, caused in the 19th century by the migration of people from the countryside to work in the growing urban factories

CHAPTER 8

communism—a political belief that the working class should take control of the government and the economy in order to create a classless society

factory system—the production of goods in factories instead of in workers' homes

imperialism—policies common among strong countries aimed at gaining social, economic, and political control over weaker ones

Industrial Revolution—the development of power-driven machinery and the factory system that began in the late 18th century and spread rapidly in the 19th century, especially in Europe and North America

interchangeable parts—a system in which individual pieces of a product are made exactly the same way and can be exchanged with one another

labor union—an organization of workers that aims to protect and further workers' interests in such matters as wages and working conditions

laissez-faire—a French term meaning "let do" or "let alone"; the belief that a government should interfere as little as possible in a nation's economy

Marxian—based on the ideas of Karl Marx

protectorate—an area that a nation controls but does not rule directly

raw materials—substances that need to be processed in some way before they become useful, such as metal ores and cotton bolls

socialism—a political belief that favors government ownership of major industries

sphere of influence—an area that a nation does not rule but over which it has enough power and influence to further its interests

trade barrier—any restriction on trade (such as a tariff or quota) between nations or regions

utopian—having to do with the idea of a perfect society. The word comes from Thomas More's book *Utopia* (1516), which described such a society.

CHAPTER 9

armistice—in a war, an agreement to stop fighting, either temporarily or permanently

mandate—in general, an official order or authorization. Under the League of Nations after World War I, an authorization for an Allied nation to govern a colony of a defeated nation.

militarism—the belief that expansion of a nation's armed forces is essential to its power and prestige. In some nations, militarism also means the belief that the armed forces should have political power.

mobilize—to make a country's armed forces ready for immediate action

ratify—to confirm something officially, such as a treaty, constitution, or presidential appointment

reparations—the payment of damages, especially the payment exacted from a nation defeated in a war by the victorious nation or nations

self-determination—the ability of a people to choose their own political status. For example, people of the same ethnic group may wish to have their own nation rather then be a colony or be divided among two or more nations.

ultimatum—a demand that, if not agreed to, will lead to some kind of punishment

war of attrition—a conflict in which neither side can make any headway; instead, both sides are slowly worn down

CHAPTER 10

collective farm—in Communist countries, a large, government-run farm consisting of many families

demagogue—a political leader who plays on people's prejudices and fears in order to gain power

depression—a severe, long-term downturn in the economy of a country or region. In a depression, production falls off sharply and unemployment rises.

fascism—a system of government that demands total obedience to a dictator, uses force and censorship to eliminate opposition, preaches an extreme form of nationalism, and glorifies militarism

indoctrination—teaching meant to favor or impose a particular point of view

inflation—a general rise in prices of goods and services over an extended period of time

totalitarianism—government control over all aspects of life in a nation by means of force and terror

CHAPTER 11

anti-Semitism—prejudice against or hatred of Jews

appeasement—giving in to an aggressor's demands in hopes of preventing further aggression or a war

concentration camp—an encampment surrounded by barbed or electrified wire in which a large number of prisoners are confined; especially the camps used in Nazi Germany to imprison Jews, Slavs, political opponents, and others under inhuman and sometimes deadly conditions. Some were **death camps**, designed to kill all inmates.

genocide—the mass murder of a religious, political, or ethnic group

Holocaust—the Nazis' deliberate extermination of more than 6 million Jews and millions of other people before and during World War II

CHAPTER 12

cold war—the conflict between the United States and the Soviet Union that involved such tactics as military alliances, wars carried out by third parties, espionage, threats, and propaganda but that avoided direct military action

containment—preventing a hostile country or group of countries from expanding by such means as alliances and ready military power

deterrence—the policy of building up a nation's military power to discourage attack by another nation

quarantine—the forced isolation of a person or group

satellite nation—a supposedly independent country that is controlled by a more powerful country

CHAPTER 13

apartheid—South Africa's former policy of separation of the races

partition—in general, to divide an area into separate parts. In global politics, to divide a territory or nation into separate political units.

viceroy—the governor of the colony of a monarchy (the word means "in place of the king")

Zionism—the political movement to set up a Jewish homeland in Palestine

CHAPTER 14

caliph—a successor of Muhammad as leader of Islam

caste system—a rigid ordering of social classes. In India, one of the oldest caste systems still persists to a great extent.

covenant—a solemn agreement

crucifixion—an ancient Roman method of putting a criminal to death by nailing or tying him or her to a cross. The Bible describes how Jesus Christ was condemned as a criminal and crucified.

diaspora—a scattering of a people from their homeland. The **Diaspora** (with capital D) refers to the Jews who settled in many different parts of the world after being exiled from ancient Palestine.

disciple—a follower and supporter of an admired person, especially a religious leader

guru—in Hinduism, a holy man who devotes his life to meditation and prayer and will give advice to those who ask

hajj—a pilgrimage to Mecca, the holy city of Islam

Hegira—the journey of Muhammad and his supporters from Mecca to Medina

karma—in Hinduism, the sum total of a person's actions in this life, for good or bad. With **reincarnation**, karma is believed to determine the level of a person's next life; for example, as an animal or as a more fortunate human being

monotheism—a belief in one God

mosque—a Muslim house of worship

nirvana—in Buddhism, the highest state of mind to which humans can aspire: oneness with the universe

polytheism—a belief in more than one god

reincarnation—In Hinduism, the belief that humans are born into another life on earth after they die in their present life. Depending on one's actions in this life, one may be reborn into a higher or lower level. (See also **karma**.)

tenet—a basic principle or belief

theocracy—literally, a state ruled by God; in practice, a state ruled by religious leaders in accordance with their beliefs

CHAPTER 15

multinational corporation—a business firm that operates in multiple countries

refugee—a person forced by war, persecution, or other dangers to flee his or her homeland

Index

Acknowledgments

We gratefully acknowledge the permission of the following persons and organizations to reproduce the prints and photographs in this book. Each bold number refers to the page number where the image appears in this book.

29: Lucas Granach/Corbis **30:** Gustavo Tomsich/Corbis **32:** Time-Life Pictures/Getty Images **40:** Corbis **61:** Stock Montage **64:** North Wind **67:** Bettmann/Corbis **70:** Corbis **71:** Time-Life Pictures/Getty Images **86:** Corbis **92:** Bettmann/Corbis **100:** Corbis **101:** Corbis **104:** Bettmann/Corbis **108:** Bettmann/Corbis **111:** Hulton-Deutsch/Corbis **119:** Hulton-Deutsch/Corbis **129:** Bettmann/Corbis **131:** Corbis **137:** Hulton Archive/Getty Images **153:** Sam Sallinen/AP/Wide World Photos **155:** NASA **157:** Erich Hartmann/Magnum **158:** Reuters NewMedia Inc./Corbis

SOL Practice Test I

1. The area shaded darker on the map shows the location of which empire in 1500?
   a. Incan
   b. Mayan
   c. Songhai
   d. Aztec

PACIFIC OCEAN

Cuzco•

Andes Mts.

ATLANTIC OCEAN

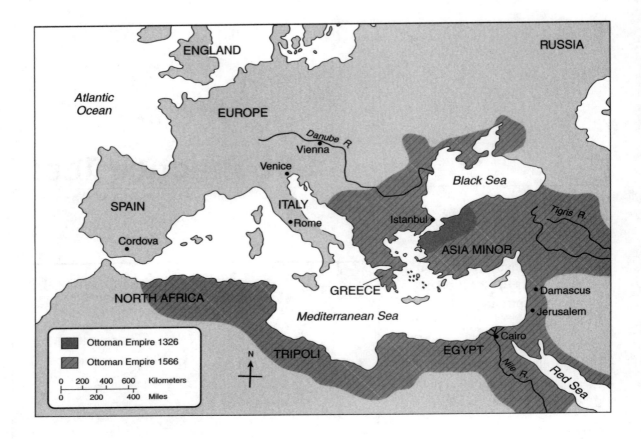

2. The darker shaded area on the map shows the location of which empire in 1326?

   f. Roman

   g. Ottoman

   h. Byzantine

   j. Mongol

3. What effect did the Black Death have on the Roman Catholic Church?

   a. The terror of the plague strengthened the role of the Church in the everyday life of people throughout Western Europe.

   b. The Church was replaced in some places by Judaism and in other places by Islam.

   c. This catastrophe undermined some Europeans' faith in the Church.

   d. The Church withstood the challenges presented by the plague without major difficulties.

4. Renaissance thinking drew heavily on the ideas of which two ancient civilizations?

   f. China and Japan

   g. Mexico and Peru

   h. Ghana and Mali

   j. Greece and Rome

5. The Renaissance spread which philosophy across Europe, starting in the south and moving northward?

   a. mercantilism

b. humanism

c. Protestantism

d. usury

6. The statement, "The just shall live by faith" is associated with which Reformation leader?

f. Martin Luther

g. John Calvin

h. Henry VIII

j. Elizabeth I

7. "Predestination" was a fundamental principle taught by

a. Martin Luther.

b. John Calvin.

c. Henry VIII.

d. Elizabeth I.

8. Invention of the modern, movable-type printing press is attributed to

f. Johannes Gutenberg.

g. King James I.

h. Johannes Kepler.

j. Isaac Newton.

9. Which statement *best* describes the goal of the Society of Jesus (Jesuits)?

a. to spread Spanish influence throughout the New World

b. to counter the influence of the Anglican Church in England

c. to foster communication between Protestants and Catholics

d. to spread Catholic doctrine around the world

10. Some historians have described Columbus's voyages to the islands of the Caribbean as the beginning of an "American holocaust." What is meant by that?

f. Spanish explorations of the Americas created a new way for Europeans to view the world.

g. Columbus and his men brought the use of fire to the Americas.

h. Spanish cruelty and diseases decimated the Native American populations of the Caribbean region.

j. The Spanish used silver from the Americas to finance a larger army and navy.

11. The term "Middle Passage" refers to the

a. middle leg of the Triangular Trade, bringing African slaves across the Atlantic Ocean to the Americas.

b. middle route across the Atlantic Ocean, used by merchants to reach Brazil most quickly.

c. middle stage in establishing the slave trade, bringing Africans to Europe for sale.

d. shortest land route across the New World territories, in Central America.

12. Which European nation is not correctly matched with its major colonial holdings in the 17th and 18th centuries?

f. Spain—Central America, the west coast of South America, much of western and southern North America

g. Portugal—the part of South America that is now Brazil

h. England—the eastern coast of North America

j. France—the part of South America that is now Peru

13. The pattern of trade shown on the map below is most often called the
   a. trade winds.
   b. search for the Middle Passage.
   c. Columbian Exchange.
   d. Silk Road.

14. The theory of mercantilism called for imports of gold and silver into Europe in the 17th century. The most immediate effect of these imports was
   f. increased industrial production.
   g. dramatic increases in unemployment.
   h. agricultural shortages.
   j. increased European trade.

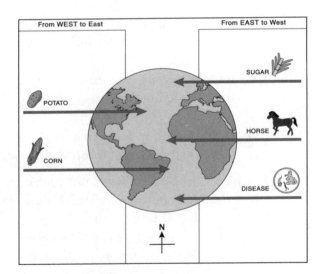

15. In the 1500s, military leaders called shoguns ruled
   a. China.
   b. Korea.
   c. Vietnam.
   d. Japan.

16. Peter the Great is remembered *most* for
   f. promoting the Russian Orthodox Church.
   g. defeating Sweden in war.
   h. establishing democracy in Russia.
   j. modernizing Russian government and society.

17. On the timeline on page 185, which revolution is located between the Glorious Revolution and the French Revolution?
   a. Industrial Revolution
   b. Scientific Revolution
   c. American Revolution
   d. Russian Revolution

18. Copernicus was correct with his heliocentric model of the solar system. However, his model was *incorrect* in which of the following ways?
   f. He claimed that the earth was the center of the solar system.
   g. He stated that the planets traveled in perfect circles.
   h. He denied that the planets moved.
   j. He calculated that the solar system is much larger than it is.

1500————————1600————————1700————————1800————————1900

Spain and Portugal   The Netherlands   _____

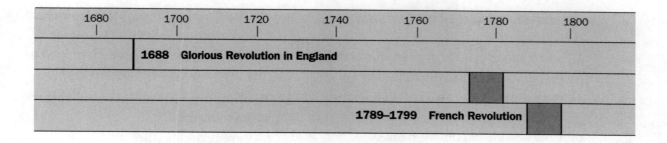

| 1680 | 1700 | 1720 | 1740 | 1760 | 1780 | 1800 |

1688 Glorious Revolution in England

1789–1799 French Revolution

19. Which philosopher argued that "people are naturally good, but society corrupts them"?

   a. Jean-Jacques Rousseau
   b. John Locke
   c. Thomas Hobbes
   d. Thomas Jefferson

   f. 1
   g. 3
   h. 5
   j. 10

20. The timeline at the bottom of page 184 shows the dominant European trading nations from 1500 to 1900. What nation belongs in the blank space.

   f. France
   g. Greece
   h. Russia
   j. Great Britain

21. John Locke's argument that life, liberty, and property were natural rights became a central theme of the

   a. *Spirit of the Laws.*
   b. *Declaration of Independence.*
   c. Congress of Vienna.
   d. *Communist Manifesto.*

22. From studying the map of South America, how many South American nations became independent between 1790 and 1828?

23. An immediate cause of the French Revolution was
    a. a bad harvest and high prices for bread.
    b. the storming of the Bastille.
    c. the French declaration of war against Austria.
    d. Louis XIV's becoming King of France.

24. Thirty-nine German states maintained their independence until the middle of what century?
    f. 17th
    g. 18th
    h. 19th
    j. 20th

25. Napoleon attempted to achieve all of the following *except*
    a. independence for Haiti.
    b. increased French nationalism.
    c. French control of Europe.
    d. an improved legal system.

26. Which event led directly to the Congress of Vienna?
    f. unification of Germany under Bismarck
    g. storming of the Bastille
    h. independence of the American colonies
    j. defeat of Napoleon in 1814

27. Which statement *best* shows how the Congress of Vienna "turned back the hands of time"?
    a. The Congress promoted a stronger France and Germany.
    b. The Congress promoted balance of power and suppressed democracy.
    c. The Congress promoted democracy and suppressed conservatism.
    d. The Congress restored Napoleon to power and promoted dictatorship.

28. The Industrial Revolution came first to which industries?
    f. mining and textiles
    g. steel production and brewing
    h. home building and fine furniture
    j. automobile and steam engine production

29. The words "Workingmen of all countries, unite" were intended to
    a. create support for labor unions.
    b. foster greater cooperation among workers at different levels.
    c. begin a Communist revolution.
    d. ease tensions in the new capitalist system.

30. Refer to the map on page 187 of Africa in 1914. Which number represents a major imperialist holding of France in Africa at that time?
    f. 1
    g. 2
    h. 3
    j. 4

31. The mining problem that was solved in the early 18th century by Thomas Newcomen was
    a. improving air quality for the miners.
    b. inventing sharper cutting tools to make deeper mines in a shorter time.
    c. pumping water out of the mines.
    d. creating a system for miners to keep in touch with managers on the surface.

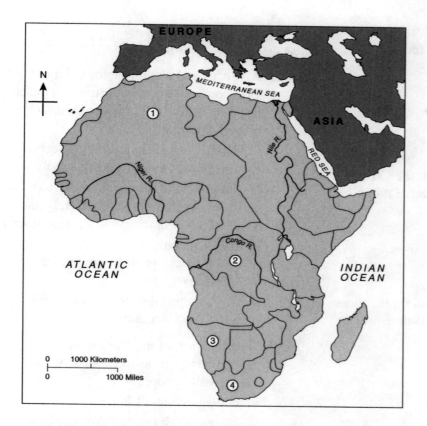

32. What were the views of most textile manufacturers in the 19th century about woman and children working in their factories?

    f. Women and children were considered to be too weak to run the machines.

    g. Women and children were desired for their small hands and their willingness to work for low wages.

    h. Women and children were forbidden to enter the textile factories due to insurance regulations.

    j. Women were desired for textile factory work but children were not.

33. What determined the wages of 18th- and 19th-century factory workers in *most* industries?

    a. the lowest wage at which the jobs could be filled

    b. the labor contract worked out by a union

    c. the fair wage theory of Robert Owen

    d. the theory of socialism as interpreted by the factory owners

34. The British discovered that they could dominate trade with China in the 19th century by sending which product to China?

    f. tea

    g. textiles

    h. grains

    j. opium

35. The unification of Germany came about through the efforts of

    a. Cavour.

    b. Bismarck.

    c. Garibaldi.

    d. Kaiser Wilhelm.

36. Which writer's works became the basis for communism around the world?
    f. Robert Owen
    g. Karl Marx
    h. Adam Smith
    j. Andrew Carnegie

37. Which British imperial possession, referred to as the "Jewel in the Crown," finally won independence in 1947?
    a. China
    b. Canada
    c. Singapore
    d. India

38. Which African nation put up the most *successful* resistance to 19th-century European imperialism?
    f. Senegal
    g. Kenya
    h. Ethiopia
    j. Sudan

39. Utopian socialists and Marxian socialists disagreed on the
    a. desirability of a worker revolution.
    b. injustices of capitalism.
    c. importance of the factory system.
    d. value of workers in producing goods.

40. The nation that contributed the largest number of technological improvements in the 18th and early 19th centuries was
    f. France.
    g. the United States.
    h. Germany.
    j. Great Britain.

41. The Boxer Rebellion took place in which country?
    a. the United States
    b. China
    c. India
    d. South Vietnam

42. Alliances and commitments enlarged the 1914 conflict between Austria and Serbia into World War I. Which commitments played a part in this?
    f. Russia's promise to defend Serbia and Great Britain's promise to defend Belgium
    g. Serbia's promise to defend Belgium and Russia's promise to defend Austria
    h. Italy's promise to defend Germany and Russia's promise to defend Austria
    j. the U. S. promise to defend France and Great Britain

43. Which action of the Bolshevik government was most popular with the Russian people?
    a. collectivizing all farms
    b. taking Russia out of World War I
    c. establishing a network of secret police
    d. giving all power to Lenin

44. Assess the authenticity of this note to Franz Joseph Haydn:

    My dearest Franz,

    I applaud your excellent oratorio The Creation. *You have advanced the field of religious music significantly.*
    Yours,
    Adolf Hitler

    f. There is no basis for judging whether the note is authentic.
    g. The note is probably fake because Hitler took no interest in music.
    h. The note is probably fake because Haydn did not write religious music.
    j. The note is probably fake because

Haydn died long before Hitler was born.

45. Which conclusion is *most* reasonable from the following table of World War I casualties?

Country	Number of Soldiers Killed
Great Britain	approximately 1 million
France	between 1 and 2 million
Germany	between 1 and 2 million
Russia	over 5 million
United States	115,000

   a. Due to its relatively small number of casualties, the United States had little interest in the terms of the Versailles Treaty.

   b. The defeated nations had drastically greater numbers of casualties than the victorious nations.

   c. Great Britain and France were likely to be more interested in revenge against Germany than the United States was.

   d. Though there were many casualties of World War I, the effects of the war passed quickly from the minds of Europeans.

46. Which of the major powers did not ratify the Versailles Treaty and its provision of a League of Nations?

   f. France

   g. Great Britain

   h. Italy

   j. the United States

47. After World War I, the mandate system provided temporary government for

   a. nations conquered by the Germans and Italians during the war.

   b. former German colonies and the old Ottoman empire.

   c. territories in the new Soviet Union.

   d. a Jewish homeland in Palestine.

48. The following factors helped to cause the worldwide depression of the 1930s *except*

   f. high protective tariffs.

   g. excessive expansion of credit.

   h. U.S. dominance of the global economy.

   j. totalitarian regimes in the Soviet Union and Italy.

49. Aggressive actions by the Japanese government in the 1930s and early 1940s were *primarily* motivated by

   a. a racist ideology.

   b. Japanese citizens' hatred for the United States.

   c. friendship with Nazi Germany.

   d. a need for raw materials.

50. Which of the following actions best represents the strategy of appeasement?

   f. creation of high tariff barriers by many nations in the 1920s

   g. forced collective farming in the Soviet Union

   h. British and French acceptance of the Munich Agreement

   j. U.S. Senate opposition to the Versailles Treaty

51. How did the United States participate in World War II before the Japanese attack on Pearl Harbor?

    a. limited its participation to criticism of Japanese imperialism

    b. provided war materials, including naval destroyers, to the British

    c. attacked German forces in Italy to relieve German pressure on the Soviet Union

    d. flew bombing missions over Germany

52. The map below depicts the movements of the armed forces of the United States and its allies in the Pacific from 1942 to 1945. What does it show about the U.S. strategy to defeat Japan?

    f. The United States invaded Japan first, then Japan's conquered territories.

    g. The invasion of Japan was never planned by the United States. Destruction of Japan's conquered territories by itself would guarantee U.S. success.

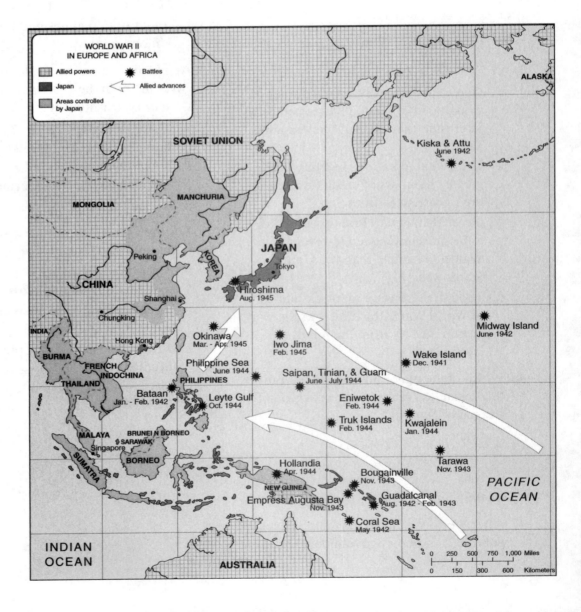

h. The United States sought to avoid Japanese naval forces because Pearl Harbor had proved the Japanese fleet to be superior to the U.S. fleet.

j. U.S. forces destroyed Japanese naval and ground forces through much of the Pacific, established strategic bases, and prepared for the invasion of Japan.

53. The three maps below show Communist-ruled areas of the world at three points in time: in 1917, in 1990, and today. Which is the correct sequence of the maps?

a. Map A, then Map B, then Map C
b. Map B, then Map A, then Map C
c. Map C, then Map B, then Map A
d. Map A, then Map C, then Map B

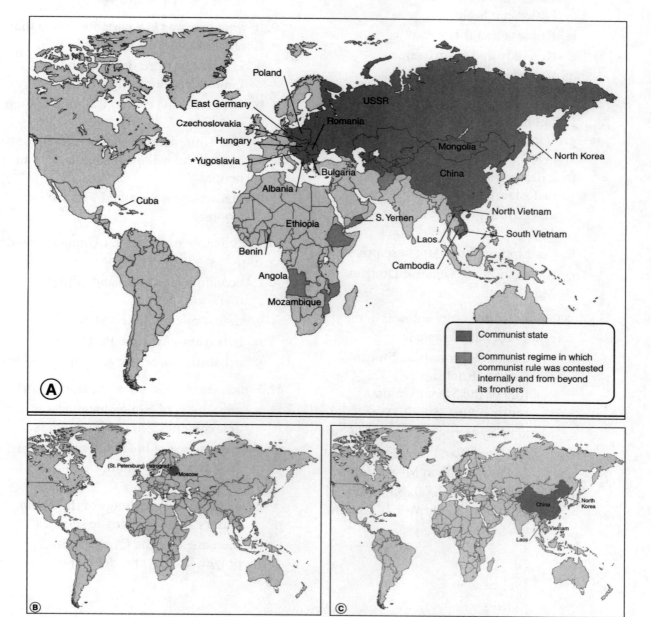

54. Which international crisis brought the world to the brink of nuclear war?

    f. the Vietnam War

    g. the building of the Berlin Wall

    h. the Algerian war of independence

    j. the Cuban Missile Crisis

55. Which pair of leaders is most closely associated with the end of the cold war?

    a. Hitler and Stalin

    b. Roosevelt and Truman

    c. Kennedy and Khrushchev

    d. Reagan and Gorbachev

56. Which account of the fighting in the Philippines in World War II would probably have the greatest accuracy and least bias?

    f. a description by a professional historian writing in the 1990s

    g. an account given by a U.S. soldier in 1945

    h. descriptions from Japanese prisoners

    j. the memoirs of General Douglas MacArthur

57. Which series of events below is in the correct historical sequence?

    a. Protestant Reformation, French Revolution, English Civil War, collapse of the Soviet Union

    b. French Revolution, World War II, Mandate System, Cuban Missile Crisis

    c. English Civil War, French Revolution, World War II, Cuban Missile Crisis

    d. English Civil War, collapse of the Soviet Union, World War II, Cuban Missile Crisis

58. India was partitioned at independence due to

    f. disagreements between Gandhi and the British government.

    g. conflict between Hindus and Muslims.

    h. differences between British and French colonial policies.

    j. the effects of World War II.

59. In what way was U.S participation in the Korean War unusual?

    a. U.S. troops were fighting under United Nations authority.

    b. It was the first case of U.S. intervention in Asia.

    c. The United States was involved against the will of the South Korean people.

    d. U.S. troops were allied with Chinese troops.

60. The collapse of the Soviet Union resulted from

    f. economic problems and ethnic divisions.

    g. defeat by the United States.

    h. betrayal by Warsaw Pact allies.

    j. exhaustion of Soviet natural resources.

61. Which set of beliefs *best* fits Buddhism?

    a. sacredness of all life; happiness is detachment from worldly desires

    b. importance of holy men called gurus; gods Brahma, Vishnu, and Shiva; caste system

    c. emphasis on teachings of the Torah; dietary rules; synagogue services

    d. sacredness of the Qur'an; faith, prayer, fasting, and the hajj

62. Look at the map below. The shaded area shows the current geographic distribution of which religion?

   f. Hinduism
   g. Buddhism
   h. Christianity
   j. Islam

63. Which statement best describes the effects of new communications technology, including the Internet, on developing nations?

   a. Developing nations have lagged behind the developed nations in access to this valuable new technology.
   b. Developing nations have moved toward greater equality with developed nations as a result of Internet use.

   c. Developing nations have little use for advanced communications technology.
   d. No conclusions regarding current Internet access in developing countries can be drawn.

64. Which of the following groups is the *clearest* example of religion as a dividing force in a region of the world?

   f. Protestantism, Judaism, and Catholicism in North America
   g. Shintoism and Buddhism in Japan
   h. Catholicism and tribal faiths in Argentina
   j. Hinduism and Islam in India and Pakistan

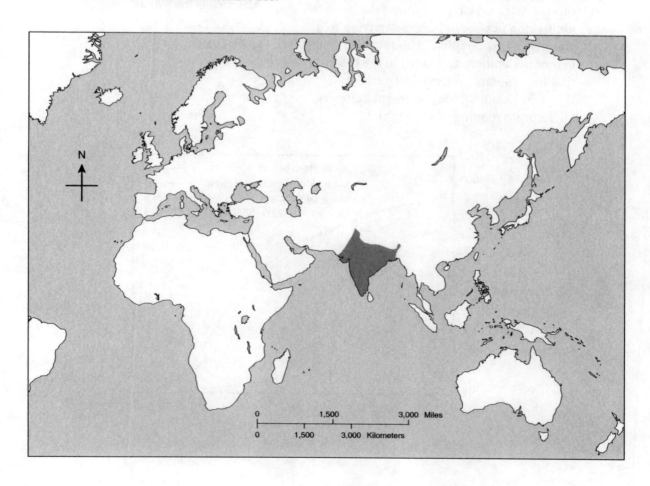

65. In the 1990s, the majority Hutu were in conflict with the Tutsi minority in
    a. Armenia.
    b. South Africa.
    c. Rwanda.
    d. Zambia.

66. Which continent or continents have been most seriously affected by the acid rain problem?
    f. Europe and North America
    g. Australia and Antarctica
    h. Africa and Asia
    j. South America

67. The graph below is a scientific projection of the possible impact of the HIV virus on countries in Africa. It shows the probability of a new-born baby's surviving to a given age. It shows that probability (a) *before* the epidemic, and (b) in the case that the epidemic infected 50 percent of the population. Which statement below is an accurate reading of the graph?

a. An HIV epidemic in a country is not likely to change the probability of a baby there reaching the age of 50.

b. If the HIV infection rate in a country reaches 50 percent, no one there will survive.

c. If the HIV infection rate reaches 50 percent in a country, both men and women there will have less than a 10 percent probability of surviving to the age of 50.

d. The HIV infection rate has no impact on the population of a country even at high levels of infection.

68. The agreement to work toward a single market without trade barriers in North America is known as
    f. NAFTA.
    g. WTO.
    h. NATO.
    j. IRA.

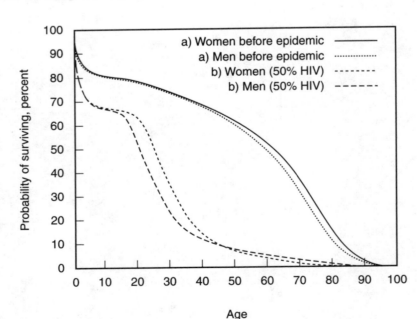

69. Which number on the top map represents the nation of Kenya?

   a. 1

   b. 2

   c. 3

   d. 4

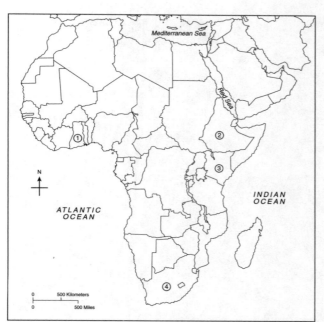

70. Which number on the map below represents the nation of Iran?

   f. 1

   g. 2

   h. 3

   j. 4

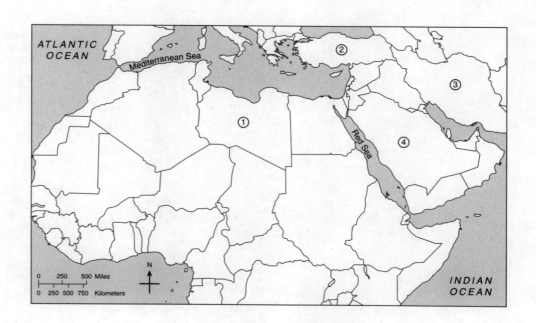

1. The area shaded darker on the map
   shows the location of which empire in
   1500?
   a. Incan
   b. Mayan
   c. Aztec
   d. Songhai

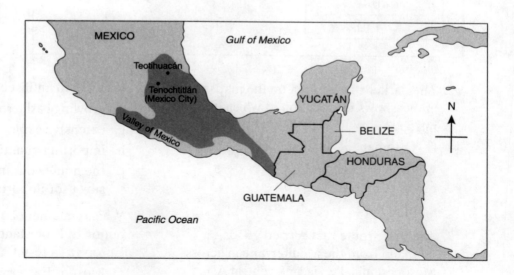

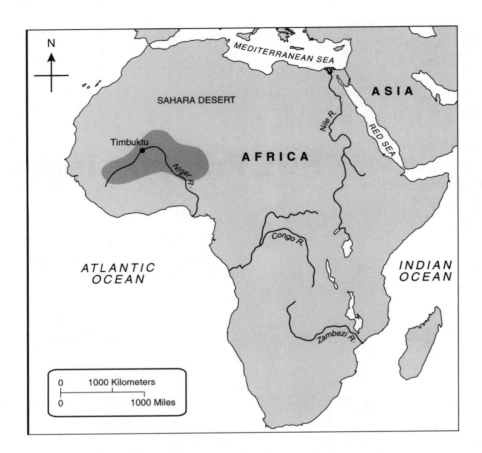

2. The darker shaded area on the map above shows the location of which empire in 1500?
   f. Ottoman
   g. Persian
   h. Mayan
   j. Songhai

3. The trade route that carried goods overland from the Mediterranean across Mesopotamia, Persia, and central Asia to China and back was called the
   a. trans-Saharan Caravan Route.
   b. Indian Ocean Trade Network.
   c. Mediterranean Trade Network.
   d. Silk Road.

4. Which of the following is *not* consistent with a mercantilist economic policy?
   f. growing cash crops in colonies
   g. extensive exploration and conquest
   h. importing quantities of gold and silver
   j. the home country paying gold and silver for imported goods

5. Which statement best describes the distribution of Protestants and Catholics in Europe as a result of the Reformation?
   a. Most of Eastern Europe became Protestant.
   b. The Reformation split Europe into equal parts of Jewish, Catholic, and Protestant lands.
   c. Northern Europe remained Catholic, while most of Southern Europe became Protestant.

d. Much of Northern Europe became Protestant, while Southern Europe remained mostly Catholic.

6. Which of these proved *most* deadly to the Caribs, Aztecs, and Incas in the 15th and 16th centuries?

f. Spanish horses

g. European diseases

h. cannons and muskets

j. their use of tobacco

7. Which of the following was a lasting result of the Spanish conquests in the Americas?

a. establishment of peaceful relations among the European powers

b. creation of a social class system that gave preference to Spanish heritage

c. a permanent alliance of Peru with Mexico

d. a shorter route for European trade with Asia

8. Which ruling group spread Islam to India and established an empire supported by profitable coastal trade?

f. Ottomans

g. Mughals

h. shoguns

j. Portuguese

9. On the map below of the Triangular Trade, which group of products should be placed below arrow #3?

a. sugar, molasses, and cotton

b. captured Africans and gold

c. captured Africans, manufactured goods, and molasses

d. Native-American arts and crafts

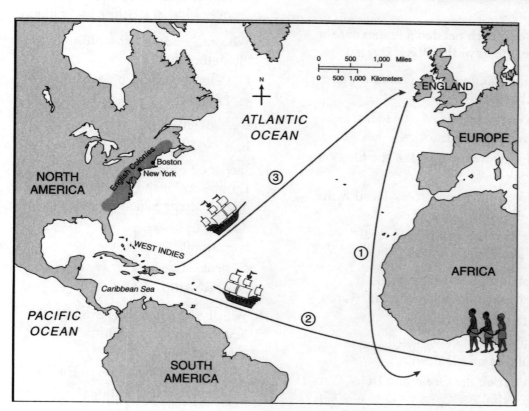

10. In addition to astronomy, major scientific breakthroughs in the 17th and 18th centuries took place in
    f. anesthesia, surgery, and public health.
    g. architecture, city planning, and engineering.
    h. botany, genetics, and zoology.
    j. anatomy and physics.

11. What was the primary reason that the Catholic Church persecuted some important 17th-century scientists?
    a. The Church opposed all science not being done by Catholic scholars.
    b. Revolutionary new views of the universe clashed with fundamental Church teachings.
    c. Church leaders failed to see the significance of the new ideas about the universe and humankind's place in it.
    d. The Church needed a scapegoat for the effects of the Black Death.

12. Voltaire's famous work *Candide* is best described as
    f. an encyclopedia of new ideas, inventions, and stories.
    g. a long, gloomy novel of the life of a monk.
    h. a lively adventure story, laced with philosophy.
    j. the first modern play to rival Shakespeare's plays.

13. Two philosophers who expressed opposite views of human nature were
    a. Jefferson and Locke.
    b. Hobbes and Rousseau.
    c. Voltaire and Diderot.
    d. Frederick the Great and Ben Franklin.

14. Which statement *best* describes the relationship of feudalism to royal power in Europe after 1500?
    f. Less control by feudal nobles meant more control by the monarch.
    g. The rise of feudalism after 1500 meant weakened royal power.
    h. Feudalism declined, as did the power of the kings.
    j. Church authority overcame both feudalism and royal power after 1500.

15. One reason for English trade success in the 17th and early 18th centuries was the
    a. efficient business practices of the English trading companies.
    b. worldwide use of the English language.
    c. failure of Spanish colonization efforts in America.
    d. high demand for coconut and cocoa, over which the British had a monopoly.

16. Who expressed his absolutism by saying "I am the state"?
    f. Peter the Great
    g. Louis XIV
    h. Machiavelli
    j. Henry VIII

17. Increased commerce and wealth in Europe during the 16th and 17th centuries directly strengthened the influence of the
    a. middle class.
    b. Catholic Church.
    c. peasants.
    d. universities.

18. Which of the following events is the *best* example of "evolution" toward constitutional monarchy?
    f. Glorious Revolution in England
    g. American Revolution

h. French Revolution

j. Russian Revolution

19. What was the significance of the newspaper headline "Napoleon Escapes from Elba"?

    a. The French Revolution was finally at an end.

    b. The former emperor would have to be defeated in battle once more.

    c. The Congress of Vienna was abolished.

    d. Napoleon was free from responsibility for the many wars that he caused.

20. Which event led directly to the outbreak of revolutions in Latin America?

    f. the Louisiana Purchase

    g. Napoleon's invasion of Russia

    h. sales of Voltaire's *Candide*

    j. Napoleon's conquest of Spain

21. Which paired terms conflict with each other?

    a. nationalism—patriotism

    b. anti-Semitism—Zionism

    c. science—experimentation

    d. Enlightenment—toleration

22. Which statesman *most clearly* demonstrated the ideas of Machiavelli's *The Prince*?

    f. David Lloyd George

    g. Neville Chamberlain

    h. Woodrow Wilson

    j. Otto von Bismarck

23. In 1848, revolutionaries called "liberals" took to the streets in many European countries to advocate

    a. royal monarchies.

    b. Communist states.

    c. parliamentary democracies.

    d. utopian experiments.

24. How was Robert Owen's New Lanark Mill different from other textile factories?

    f. His workers were better paid and provided for.

    g. He used only slave labor from the American colonies.

    h. The workers owned their own factory.

    j. The factory modeled all of the most efficient machines for textile production.

25. Early capitalism operated without government controls or regulation. What was this kind of capitalism called?

    a. mixed capitalism

    b. industrial capitalism

    c. American-style capitalism

    d. laissez-faire capitalism

26. Resistance to labor unions came primarily from

    f. factory owners.

    g. factory workers.

    h. rural laborers.

    j. utopian socialists.

27. The 19th-century textile and mining industries took which of the following views toward child labor?

    a. They both felt that it was unnecessary and unduly dangerous.

    b. Textile manufacturers supported it, but the mining industry opposed child labor.

    c. They petitioned governments to outlaw the employmentof children in both industries.

    d. Both industries used child labor extensively.

28. Which inventor improved the process for making steel?
    f. John Kay
    g. Eli Whitney
    h. James Hargreaves
    j. Henry Bessemer

29. During the American Civil War, Southerners hoped that Britain would support their cause. Great Britain did *not* support the South due to
    a. moral reasons, since the British had banned slavery in their colonies.
    b. economic reasons, since British cotton competed with Southern cotton.
    c. political reasons, since the British depended on U.S. support.
    d. social reasons, since Southern society had few ties to Britain.

30. Refer to the map below of Africa in 1914. Which of the numbered areas represents the major imperialist holding of Belgium?
    f. 1
    g. 2
    h. 3
    j. 4

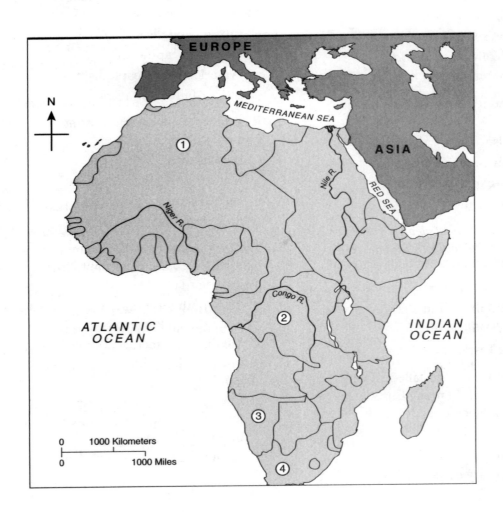

31. After 1763, the dominant colonial power in India was
    a. Great Britain.
    b. Germany.
    c. France.
    d. Italy.

32. Utopian socialism applied an optimistic viewpoint from the past to the new industrial age. Their optimism was based on the ideas of the
    f. Classical Age.
    g. Renaissance.
    h. Reformation.
    j. Enlightenment.

33. How did industrialization and urbanization affect British democracy in the 19th century?
    a. They expanded the middle class, whose men gradually obtained the right to vote.
    b. Confirming their suspicions about the poorer classes, British aristocrats suppressed democracy.
    c. Their effects on democracy were balanced by the rise of totalitarian leaders in Britain.
    d. They caused a socialist revolution, which gave all British men the right to vote.

34. The Von Schlieffen Plan was designed to avoid what possibility?
    f. a U.S. invasion of Germany
    g. Germany being left out of the war
    h. Germany having to invade Russia
    j. Germany having to fight France and Russia at the same time

35. After the assassination of Franz Ferdinand, which of the following was demanded by Austria and rejected by Serbia?
    a. Bosnian independence
    b. German sovereignty over Austria
    c. an Austrian role in the assassination investigation
    d. Russian participation in future problems with Slavs in Austria

36. Which statement best describes World War I?
    f. Offensive strategies dominated, since there were no adequate defenses against the new weapons.
    g. A deadlock on the Western Front forced a long war of attrition.
    h. There were numerous opportunities for German victory that were ignored by the German generals.
    j. Severe weather in Russia was decisive in defeating the Germans.

37. Which one of the "Big Three" proposed the Fourteen Points?
    a. Georges Clemenceau of France
    b. David Lloyd George of Britain
    c. Woodrow Wilson of the United States
    d. Benito Mussolini of Italy

38. Areas governed under the "mandate system" after World War I included parts of the old Ottoman empire and
    f. former German colonies.
    g. French territory in North Africa, including Algeria.
    h. Russian territory lost to the Germans in the war.
    j. Germany and Austria.

39. Which factor contributed *most strongly* to the rise of fascist dictatorships in Europe?
    a. antiwar feeling in the United States
    b. worldwide depression
    c. anticommunism in Italy
    d. Zionism

40. Why did President Franklin Roosevelt call December 7, 1941, "a date that will live in infamy"?
    f. It was the date of the dropping of the first atomic bomb.
    g. It was the date of the Japanese sneak attack on Pearl Harbor.
    h. It was the date that the U.S. government first learned about the Nazi Holocaust.
    j. It was the date of the defeat of U.S. forces at the Kasserine Pass in North Africa.

41. Which book laid out the economic theory for communism?
    a. *The Wealth of Nations*
    b. *Mein Kampf*
    c. *Profiles in Courage*
    d. *Das Kapital*

42. What experience did Hitler have in common with Napoleon?
    f. escape from exile and return to power
    g. military defeats in Russia
    h. persecution of the Jews of Europe
    j. betrayal by several of his closest associates

43. At the end of World War II in 1945, which countries had atomic weapons?
    a. China, the Soviet Union, Britain, and the United States
    b. the Soviet Union, Britain, and the United States
    c. the Soviet Union and the United States
    d. only the United States

44. Which nation on the map on the next page was the site of a 1994 genocide costing the lives of over 800,000 people?
    f. 1
    g. 2
    h. 3
    j. 4

45. Which alliance *best* demonstrated the proverb "The enemy of my enemy is my friend"?
    a. Franklin Roosevelt with Joseph Stalin
    b. Harry Truman with Winston Churchill
    c. Franklin Roosevelt with Winston Churchill
    d. Adolf Hitler with Benito Mussolini

46. The primary purpose of the Berlin Wall was to
    f. make Berlin easier to defend against NATO attack.
    g. reduce U.S. influences in the Eastern Zone of Berlin.
    h. keep West Berliners from moving to East Berlin.
    j. keep East Berliners from leaving East Germany.

47. A million deaths and disruption of the entire nation of Cambodia is blamed on
    a. Richard Nixon.
    b. Ho Chi Minh.
    c. Mao Zedong.
    d. Pol Pot.

48. Anti-Semitism is most directly associated with which genocide?

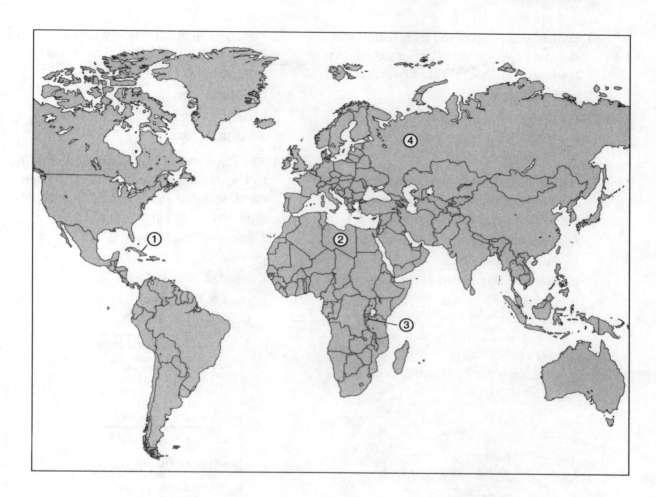

f. the Holocaust

g. Rwanda massacres

h. "ethnic cleansing" in Bosnia

j. liquidation of the kulaks of the Soviet Union

49. Under the Truman Doctrine, the United States sought to stop the spread of communism by providing massive financial support for

a. Germany and Italy.

b. Greece and Turkey.

c. Britain and France.

d. India and China.

50. One reason Britain granted independence to India after World War II was that

f. India had made its independence a condition for supporting Britain during the war.

g. Churchill had promised eventual independence to most British possessions.

h. in 1946 Indians began a widespread war for independence.

j. in 1945 the British elected a Labour government that favored Indian independence.

51. Which nation, occupied by U.S. forces at the end of World War II, later became the leading economic power in Asia?

    a. Singapore

    b. India

    c. Japan

    d. Thailand

52. As it was designed after World War II, the United Nations' strongest arm for dealing with international conflicts was its

    f. humanitarian organizations.

    g. Security Council.

    h. General Assembly.

    j. League of Nations.

53. The most significant new weapon developed during World War II was the

    a. submarine.

    b. jet airplane.

    c. flame thrower.

    d. atom bomb.

54. The statement "From Stettin in the Baltic to Trieste in the Adriatic an iron curtain has descended across the Continent" announced the beginning of the

    f. Second World War.

    g. cold war.

    h. Cuban Missile Crisis.

    j. end of the Soviet Union.

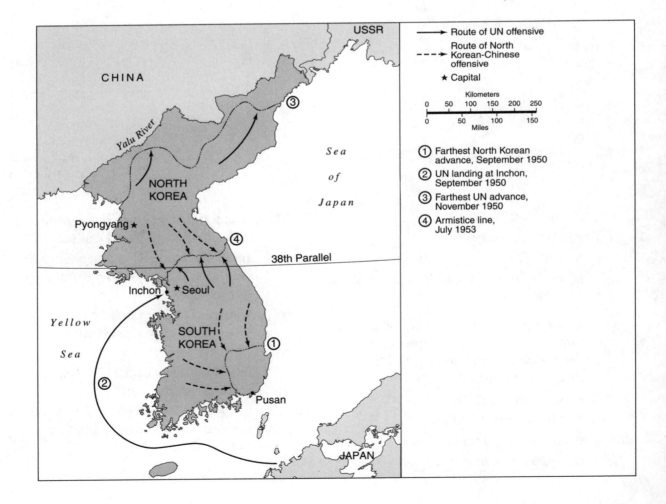

55. According to the map of the Korean War on the previous page, the line near the 38th parallel of latitude is the
    a. farthest advance northward of UN troops, in November 1950.
    b. line to which United Nations forces were forced to retreat in September 1950.
    c. cease-fire line in 1953.
    d. northern boundary of North Korea.

56. The foreign policy strategy of *deterrence* was most directly opposite to
    f. appeasement.
    g. containment.
    h. imperialism.
    j. forming alliances.

57. On the map below, which number marks the location of the oil-producing nation of Saudi Arabia?
    a. 1
    b. 2
    c. 3
    d. 4

58. Which factor complicated the independence struggle in Kenya?
    f. Kenya's European population had significant economic and political power.
    g. Kenyatta lacked experience in the movement for African independence.
    h. There were no other independence movements in Africa for the British government to contend with.
    j. The timing of Kenyan independence was out of phase with the rest of Africa.

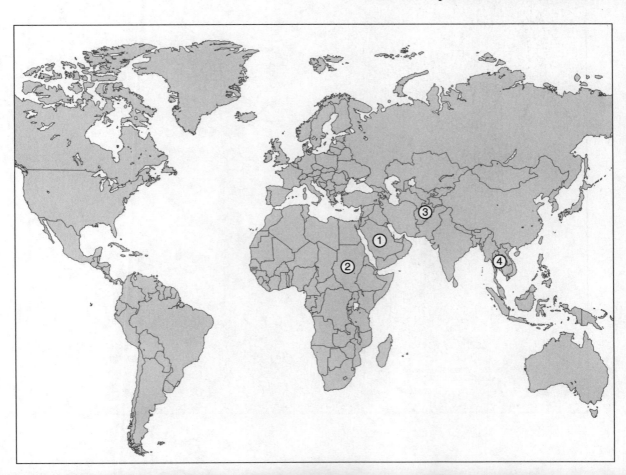

59. On the map below, which number marks the location of the nation of South Africa, where the people have struggled against apartheid?

    a. 1

    b. 2

    c. 3

    d. 4

60. What conditions of the 1990s caused Europe to become a major source of refugees for the first time since the 1940s?

    f. creation of the European Union

    g. decisions of the World Trade Organization

    h. fighting among Serbs, Bosnians, Kosovars, and Croats

    j. economic complications from acid rain

61. When did Ireland (except the northern part) become independent from Great Britain?

    a. after the French Revolution

    b. after World War I

    c. after World War II

    d. after India got its independence

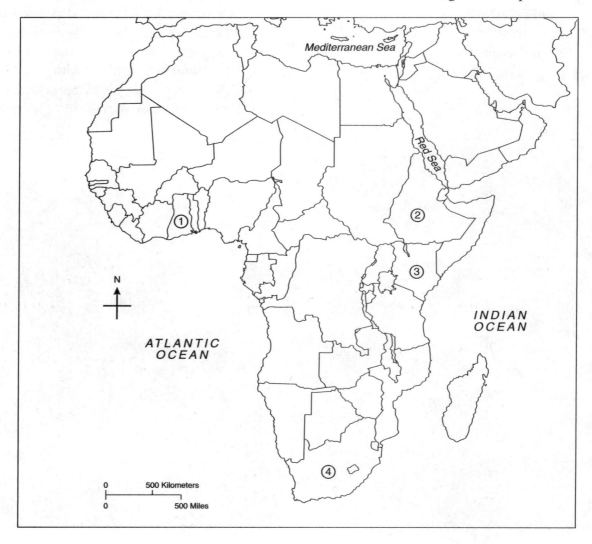

62. Look at the map below. The shaded area shows the current geographic-population distribution of which religion?

    f. Hinduism

    g. Buddhism

    h. Christianity

    j. Islam

63. Which set of beliefs fits Hinduism?

    a. sacredness of all life; happiness is detachment from worldly desires

    b. importance of holy men called gurus; gods Brahma, Vishnu, and Shiva; caste system

    c. emphasis on the teachings of the Torah; dietary laws, synagogue services

    d. sacredness of the Qur'an; faith, prayer, fasting, and the hajj

64. Abraham, Moses, and King Solomon all played a part in the

    f. conflict between the two major sects of Islam: Shi'a and Sunni.

    g. spread of Buddhism and Hinduism into the Middle East.

    h. rise of the Hebrews of the Old Testament.

    j. conquest of Hebrews by the Romans during the time of Julius Caesar.

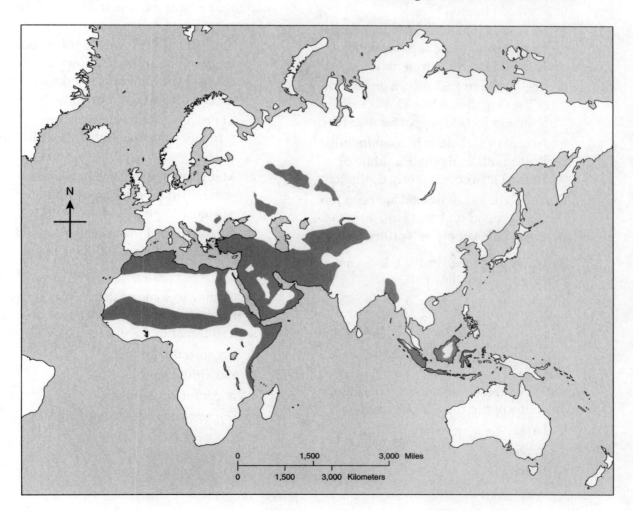

65. Which religious leader is *misplaced* in time on the timeline below?

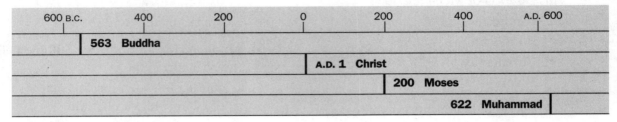

a. Buddha

b. Christ

c. Moses

d. Muhammad

66. What has been a major cause of conflict in Northern Ireland?

   f. Northern Ireland is predominantly agricultural, while the Republic of Ireland is an industrial nation.

   g. The Northern Irish fought on the side of the Germans in World War I, while Southern Ireland supported the French.

   h. Northern Ireland is predominantly Protestant, while the Republic of Ireland is predominantly Catholic.

   j. The Republic of Ireland has been too closely associated with Britain, in the view of the people of Northern Ireland.

67. Since independence in 1947, India has repeatedly clashed with

   a. Britain.

   b. France.

   c. Indonesia.

   d. Pakistan.

68. Which nation listed below is considered to be one of the "developing nations"?

   f. Israel

   g. Japan

   h. Ireland

   j. Nigeria

69. Which statement best describes the refugee problem at the start of the 21st century?

   a. The plight of refugees is tragic, but modern nations have shown a consistent willingness to take in people dispossessed by war.

   b. There have been relatively few refugees since the end of the cold war in 1991.

   c. Many small wars have produced some 40 million refugees with nowhere to go.

   d. Negotiations have usually resolved refugee problems following racial and ethnic conflicts.

70. According to some of their critics, the rise of multinational corporations poses a serious threat to the interests of

   f. organized religions.

   g. individual nations.

   h. corporate investors.

   j. science and technology.